Class Diagram

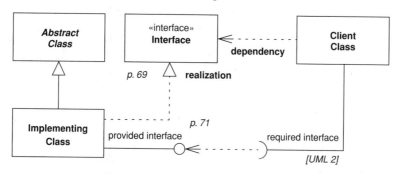

Abstract Class

«interface»
Interface

Client Class

dependency

p. 69   realization

Implementing Class

provided interface   required interface

p. 71

[UML 2]

template class *p. 81*

T

Set

bound element

Set<Integer>

Class — Class

Association Class   *p. 78*

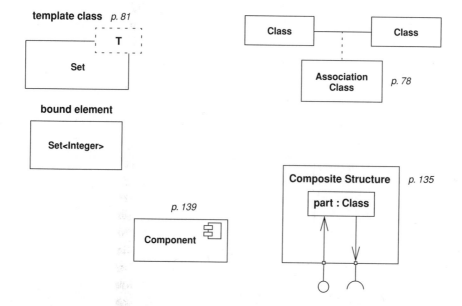

p. 139

Component

Composite Structure *p. 135*

part : Class

Communication Diagram *p. 131*

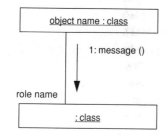

object name : class

1: message ()

role name

: class

Use Case Diagram *p. 99*

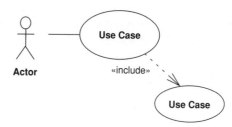

Actor

Use Case

«include»

Use Case

Praise for *UML Distilled*

"*UML Distilled* remains the best introduction to UML notation. Martin's agile and pragmatic approach hits the sweet spot, and I wholeheartedly recommend it!"

—Craig Larman
Author of *Applying UML and Patterns*

"Fowler cuts through the complexity of UML to get users started quickly."

—Jim Rumbaugh
Author and originator of UML

"Martin Fowler's *UML Distilled* is an excellent way to get started with UML. In fact for most users, *UML Distilled* contains all you need to apply UML successfully. As Martin points out, UML can be used in many ways, but the most common is as a widely recognized notation for sketching designs. This book does an excellent job of distilling the essence of UML. Highly recommended."

—Steve Cook
Software Architect
Microsoft Corporation

"Short books on UML are better than long books on UML. This is still the best short book on UML. In fact, it's the best short book on many subjects."

—Alistair Cockburn
Author and President, Humans and Technology

"The book is immensely useful, readable, and—one of its great virtues— delightfully concise for the immense scope of its subject. If you only buy one book on UML, this should be it."

—Andy Carmichael
BetterSoftwareFaster, Ltd.

"If you're using UML, this book should never be out of reach."

—John Crupi
Distinguished Engineer, Sun Microsystems
Coauthor of *Core J2EE™ Patterns*

"Anyone doing UML modeling, learning UML, reading UML, or building UML tools should have this latest edition. (I own all editions.) There is lots of good, useful information; generally, just enough to be useful, but not too much to be dry. It's a must-have reference for my bookshelf!"

—Jon Kern
Modeler

"This is a great starting point for learning the fundamentals of the UML."

—Scott W. Ambler
Author of *Agile Modeling*

"An eminently sensible description of UML and its usage, with enough humor to hold one's attention. 'The swimming metaphor no longer holds water' indeed!"

—Stephen J. Mellor
Coauthor of *Executable UML*

"This is the perfect book for those who want to use the UML but aren't interested in reading thick UML reference books and research papers. Martin Fowler selects all the critical techniques needed to use the UML for design sketches, freeing the reader from complex and rarely used UML features. Readers will find no shortage of suggestions for further reading. He gives the reader advice based on experience. It's a concise and readable book covering the essential aspects of the UML and related object-oriented concepts."

—Pavel Hruby
Microsoft Business Solutions

"Like all good software developers, Fowler improves his product with each iteration. This is the only book I consider when teaching a class involving UML or if asked to recommend one that can be used to learn it."

—Charles Ashbacher
President/CEO, Charles Ashbacher Technologies

"More books should be like *UML Distilled*—concise and readable. Martin Fowler selects the parts of UML that you need, and presents them in an easy to read style. More valuable than a mere description of the modeling language, however, is the author's insight and experience in how to use this technique to communicate and document design."

—Rob Purser
Purser Consulting, LLC.

UML Distilled
Third Edition

The Addison-Wesley Object Technology Series

Grady Booch, Ivar Jacobson, and James Rumbaugh, Series Editors
For more information, check out the series web site at www.awprofessional.com/otseries.

The Component Software Series

Clemens Szyperski, Series Editor
For more information, check out the series web site at www.awprofessional.com/csseries.

UML Distilled
Third Edition

A Brief Guide to the Standard Object Modeling Language

Martin Fowler

✦✦Addison-Wesley

Boston • San Francisco • New York • Toronto • Montreal
London • Munich • Paris • Madrid
Capetown • Sydney • Tokyo • Singapore • Mexico City

For information about buying this title in bulk quantities, or for special sales opportunities (which may include electronic versions; custom cover designs; and content particular to your business, training goals, marketing focus, or branding interests), please contact our corporate sales department at corpsales@pearsoned.com or (800) 382-3419.

For government sales inquiries, please contact governmentsales@pearsoned.com.

For questions about sales outside the U.S., please contact intlcs@pearson.com.

Visit us on the Web: informit.com/aw

Library of Congress Cataloging-in-Publication Data

Fowler, Martin, 1963–
    UML distilled : a brief guide to the standard object modeling language / Martin Fowler.—3rd ed.
        p. cm.
    Includes bibliographical references and index.
    ISBN 0-321-19368-7 (alk. paper)
    1. Object-oriented methods (Computer science)   2. Computer software—Development.   3. UML (Computer science)   I. Title.

QA76.9.O35F695 2003
005.1'7—dc22   2003057759

ISBN-13: 978-0-321-19368-1
ISBN-10: 0-321-19368-7

22   17

For Cindy

Contents

List of Figures

Foreword to
the Third Edition

Since ancient times, the most talented architects and the most gifted designers have known the law of parsimony. Whether it is stated as a paradox ("less is more"), or a koan ("Zen mind is beginner's mind"), its wisdom is timeless: Reduce everything to its essence so that form harmonizes with function. From the pyramids to the Sydney Opera House, from von Neumann architectures to UNIX and Smalltalk, the best architects and designers have strived to follow this universal and eternal principle.

Recognizing the value of shaving with Occam's Razor, when I architect and read I seek projects and books that adhere to the law of parsimony. Consequently, I applaud the book you are reading now.

You may find my last remark surprising at first. I am frequently associated with the voluminous and dense specifications that define the Unified Modeling Language (UML). These specifications allow tool vendors to implement the UML and methodologists to apply it. For seven years, I have chaired large international standardization teams to specify UML 1.1 and UML 2.0, as well as several minor revisions in between. During this time, the UML has matured in expressiveness and precision, but it has also added gratuitous complexity as a result of the standardization process. Regrettably, standardization processes are better known for design-by-committee compromises than parsimonious elegance.

What can a UML expert familiar with the arcane minutiae of the specification learn from Martin's distillation of UML 2.0? Quite a bit, as can you. To start with, Martin adroitly reduces a large and complex language into a pragmatic subset that he has proven effective in his practice. He has resisted the easy route of tacking on additional pages to the last edition of his book. As the language has grown, Martin has kept true to his goal of seeking the "fraction of UML that is most useful" and telling you just that. The fraction he refers to is the mythical 20 percent of UML that helps you do 80 percent of your work. Capturing and taming this elusive beast is no mean accomplishment!

It is even more impressive that Martin achieves this goal while writing in a wonderfully engaging conversational style. By sharing his opinions and anecdotes with us, he makes this book fun to read and reminds us that architecting and designing systems should be both creative and productive. If we pursue the parsimony koan to its full intent, we should find UML modeling projects to be as enjoyable as we found finger-painting and drawing classes in grammar school. UML should be a lightning rod for our creativity as well as a laser for precisely specifying system blueprints so that third parties can bid and build those systems. The latter is the acid test for any bona fide blueprint language.

So, while this may be a small book, it is not a trivial one. You can learn as much from Martin's approach to modeling as you can learn from his explanations of UML 2.0.

I have enjoyed working with Martin to improve the selection and correctness of the UML 2.0 language features explained in this revision. We need to keep in mind that all living languages, both natural and synthetic, must evolve or perish. Martin's choices of new features, along with your preferences and those of other practitioners, are a crucial part of the UML revision process. They keep the language vital and help it evolve via natural selection in the marketplace.

Much challenging work remains before model-driven development becomes mainstream, but I am encouraged by books like this that explain UML modeling basics clearly and apply them pragmatically. I hope you will learn from it as I have and will use your new insights to improve your own software modeling practices.

Cris Kobryn
Chair, U2 Partners' UML 2.0 Submission Team
Chief Technologist, Telelogic

Foreword to the First Edition

When we began to craft the Unified Modeling Language, we hoped that we could produce a standard means of expressing design that would not only reflect the best practices of industry, but would also help demystify the process of software system modeling. We believed that the availability of a standard modeling language would encourage more developers to model their software systems before building them. The rapid and widespread adoption of the UML demonstrates that the benefits of modeling are indeed well known to the developer community.

The creation of the UML was itself an iterative and incremental process very similar to the modeling of a large software system. The end result is a standard built on, and reflective of, the many ideas and contributions made by numerous individuals and companies from the object community. We began the UML effort, but many others helped bring it to a successful conclusion; we are grateful for their contribution.

Creating and agreeing on a standard modeling language is a significant challenge by itself. Educating the development community, and presenting the UML in a manner that is both accessible and in the context of the software development process, is also a significant challenge. In this deceptively short book, updated to reflect the most recent changes to the UML, Martin Fowler has more than met this challenge.

In a clear and friendly style, Martin not only introduces the key aspects of UML, but also clearly demonstrates the role UML plays in the development process. Along the way, we are treated to abundant nuggets of modeling insight and wisdom drawn from Martin's 12-plus years of design and modeling experience.

The result is a book that has introduced many thousands of developers to UML, whetting their appetite to further explore the many benefits of modeling with this now standard modeling language.

We recommend the book to any modeler or developer interested in getting a first look at UML and in gaining a perspective on the key role it plays in the development process.

Grady Booch
Ivar Jacobson
James Rumbaugh

Preface

I've been lucky in a lot of ways in my life; one of my great strokes of fortune was being in the right place with the right knowledge to write the first edition of this book in 1997. Back then, the chaotic world of object-oriented (OO) modeling was just beginning to unify under the Unified Modeling Language (UML). Since then, the UML has become the standard for the graphical modeling of software, not just for objects. My fortune is that this book has been the most popular book on the UML, selling more than a quarter of a million copies.

Well, that's very nice for me, but should you buy this book?

I like to stress that this is a brief book. It's not intended to give you the details on every facet of the UML, which has grown and grown over the years. My intention is to find that fraction of the UML that is most useful and tell you just that. Although a bigger book gives you more detail, it also takes longer to read. And your time is the biggest investment you'll make in a book. By keeping this book small, I've spent the time selecting the best bits to save you from having to do that selection yourself. (Sadly, being smaller doesn't mean proportionately cheaper; there is a certain fixed cost to producing a quality technical book.)

One reason to have this book is to begin to learn about the UML. Because this is a short book, it will quickly get you up to speed on the essentials of the UML. With that under your belt, you can go into more detail on the UML with the bigger books, such as the *User Guide* [Booch, UML user] or the *Reference Manual* [Rumbaugh, UML Reference].

This book can also act as a handy reference to the most common parts of the UML. Although the book doesn't cover everything, it's a lot lighter to carry around than most other UML books.

It's also an opinionated book. I've been working with objects for a long time now, and I have definite ideas about what works and what doesn't. Any book reflects the opinions of the author, and I don't try to hide mine. So if you're looking for something that has a flavor of objectivity, you might want to try something else.

Although many people have told me that this book is a good introduction to objects, I didn't write it with that in mind. If you are after an introduction to OO design, I suggest Craig Larman's book [Larman].

Many people who are interested in the UML are using tools. This book concentrates on the standard and on conventional usage of the UML and doesn't get into the details of what various tools support. Although the UML did resolve the tower of Babel of pre-UML notations, many annoying differences remain between what tools show and allow when drawing UML diagrams.

I don't say much in this book about Model Driven Architecture (MDA). Although many people consider the two to be the same thing, many developers use the UML without being interested in MDA. If you want to learn more about MDA, I would start with this book to get an overview of the UML first and then move on to a book that's more specific about MDA.

Although the main point of this book is the UML, I've also added bits of other material about techniques, such as CRC cards, that are valuable for OO design. The UML is just a part of what you need to succeed with objects, and I think that it's important to introduce you to some other techniques.

In a brief book like this, it's impossible to go into detail about how the UML relates to source code, particularly as there is no standard way of making that correspondence. However, I do point out common coding techniques for implementing pieces of the UML. My code examples are in Java and C#, as I've found that these languages are usually the most widely understood. Don't assume that I prefer those languages; I've done too much Smalltalk for that!

Why Bother with the UML?

Graphical design notations have been with us for a while. For me, their primary value is in communication and understanding. A good diagram can often help communicate ideas about a design, particularly when you want to avoid a lot of details. Diagrams can also help you understand either a software system or a business process. As part of a team trying to figure out something, diagrams both help understanding and communicate that understanding throughout a team. Although they aren't, at least yet, a replacement for textual programming languages, they are a helpful assistant.

Many people believe that in the future, graphical techniques will play a dominant role in software development. I'm more skeptical of that, but it's certainly useful to have an appreciation of what these notations can and can't do.

Of these graphical notations, the UML's importance comes from its wide use and standardization within the OO development community. The UML has become not only the dominant graphical notation within the OO world but also a popular technique in non-OO circles.

Structure of the Book

Chapter 1 gives an introduction to the UML: what it is, the different meanings it has to different people, and where it came from.

Chapter 2 talks about software process. Although this is strictly independent of the UML, I think that it's essential to understand process in order to see the context of something like the UML. In particular, it's important to understand the role of iterative development, which has been the underlying approach to process for most of the OO community.

I've organized the rest of the book around the diagram types within the UML. Chapters 3 and 4 discuss the two most useful parts of the UML: class diagrams (core) and sequence diagrams. Even though this book is slim, I believe that you can get the most value out of the UML by using the techniques that I talk about in these chapters. The UML is a large and growing beast, but you don't need all of it.

Chapter 5 goes into detail on the less essential but still useful parts of class diagrams. Chapters 6 through 8 describe three useful diagrams that shed further light on the *structure* of a system: object diagrams, package diagrams, and deployment diagrams.

Chapters 9 through 11 show three further useful *behavioral* techniques: use cases, state diagrams (although officially known as state machine diagrams, they are generally called state diagrams), and activity diagrams. Chapters 12 through 17 are very brief and cover diagrams that are generally less important, so for these, I've only provided a quick example and explanation.

The inside covers summarize the most useful parts of the notation. I've often heard people say that these covers are the most valuable part of the book. You'll probably find it handy to refer to them as you're reading some of the other parts of the book.

Changes for the Third Edition

If you have earlier editions of this book, you're probably wondering what is different and, more important, whether you should buy the new edition.

The primary trigger for the third edition was the appearance of UML 2. UML 2 has added a lot of new stuff, including several new diagram types. Even familiar diagrams have a lot of new notation, such as interaction frames in sequence diagrams. If you want to be aware of what's happened but don't want to wade through the specification (I certainly don't recommend that!), this book should give you a good overview.

I've also taken this opportunity to completely rewrite most of the book, bringing the text and examples up to date. I've incorporated much that I've learned in teaching and using the UML over the past five years. So although the spirit of this ultrathin UML book is intact, most of the words are new.

Over the years, I've worked hard to keep this book as current as is possible. As the UML has gone through its changes, I've done my best to keep pace. This book is based on the UML 2 drafts that were accepted by the relevant committee in June 2003. It's unlikely that further changes will occur between that vote and more formal votes, so I feel that UML 2 is now stable enough for my revision to go into print. I'll post information any further updates on my Web site (http://martinfowler.com).

Acknowledgments

Over many years, many people have been part of the success of this book. My first thanks go Carter Shanklin and Kendall Scott. Carter was the editor at Addison-Wesley who suggested this book to me. Kendall Scott helped me put together the first two editions, working over the text and graphics. Between them, they pulled off the impossible in getting the first edition out in an impossibly short time, while keeping up the high quality that people expect from Addison-Wesley. They also kept pushing out changes during the early days of the UML when nothing seemed stable.

Jim Odell has been my mentor and guide for much of the early part of my career. He's also been deeply involved with the technical and personal issues of making opinionated methodologists settle their differences and agree to a common standard. His contribution to this book is both profound and difficult to measure, and I bet it's the same for the UML too.

The UML is a creature of standards, but I'm allergic to standards bodies. So to know what's going on, I need a network of spies who can keep me up to date on all the machinations of the committees. Without these spies, including Conrad Bock, Steve Cook, Cris Kobryn, Jim Odell, Guus Ramackers, and Jim

Rumbaugh, I would be sunk. They've all given me useful tips and answered stupid questions.

Grady Booch, Ivar Jacobson, and Jim Rumbaugh are known as the Three Amigos. Despite the playful jibes I've given them over the years, they have given me much support and encouragement with this book. Never forget that my jabs usually sprout from fond appreciation.

Reviewers are the key to a book's quality, and I learned from Carter that you can never have too many reviewers. The reviewers of the previous editions of this book were Simmi Kochhar Bhargava, Grady Booch, Eric Evans, Tom Hadfield, Ivar Jacobson, Ronald E. Jeffries, Joshua Kerievsky, Helen Klein, Jim Odell, Jim Rumbaugh, and Vivek Salgar.

The third edition also had a fine group of reviewers:

Conrad Bock	Craig Larman
Andy Carmichael	Steve Mellor
Alistair Cockburn	Jim Odell
Steve Cook	Alan O'Callaghan
Luke Hohmann	Guus Ramackers
Pavel Hruby	Jim Rumbaugh
Jon Kern	Tim Seltzer
Cris Kobryn	

All these reviewers spent time reading the manuscript, and every one of them found at least one embarrassing howler. My sincere thanks to all of them. Any howlers that remain are entirely my responsibility. I will post an errata sheet to the books section of **martinfowler.com** when I find them.

The core team that designed and wrote the UML specification are Don Baisley, Morgan Björkander, Conrad Bock, Steve Cook, Philippe Desfray, Nathan Dykman, Anders Ek, David Frankel, Eran Gery, Øystein Haugen, Sridhar Iyengar, Cris Kobryn, Birger Møller-Pedersen, James Odell, Gunnar Övergaard, Karin Palmkvist, Guus Ramackers, Jim Rumbaugh, Bran Selic, Thomas Weigert, and Larry Williams. Without them, I would have nothing to write about.

Pavel Hruby developed some excellent Visio templates that I use a lot for UML diagrams; you can get them at **http://phruby.com**.

Many people have contacted me on the Net and in person with suggestions and questions and to point out errors. I haven't been able to keep track of you all, but my thanks are no less sincere.

The people at my favorite technical bookstore, SoftPro in Burlington, Massachusetts, let me spend many hours there looking at their stock to find how people use the UML in practice and fed me good coffee while I was there.

For the third edition, the acquisition editor was Mike Hendrickson. Kim Arney Mulcahy managed the project, as well as did the layout and clean-up of the diagrams. John Fuller, at Addison-Wesley, was the production editor, while Evelyn Pyle and Rebecca Rider helped with the copyediting and proofreading of the book. I thank them all.

Cindy has stayed with me while I persist in writing books. She then plants the proceeds in the garden.

My parents started me off with a good education, from which all else springs.

Martin Fowler
Melrose, Massachusetts
http://martinfowler.com

Chapter 1

Introduction

What Is the UML?

The Unified Modeling Language (UML) is a family of graphical notations, backed by single meta-model, that help in describing and designing software systems, particularly software systems built using the object-oriented (OO) style. That's a somewhat simplified definition. In fact, the UML is a few different things to different people. This comes both from its own history and from the different views that people have about what makes an effective software engineering process. As a result, my task in much of this chapter is to set the scene for this book by explaining the different ways in which people see and use the UML.

Graphical modeling languages have been around in the software industry for a long time. The fundamental driver behind them all is that programming languages are not at a high enough level of abstraction to facilitate discussions about design.

Despite the fact that graphical modeling languages have been around for a long time, there is an enormous amount of dispute in the software industry about their role. These disputes play directly into how people perceive the role of the UML itself.

The UML is a relatively open standard, controlled by the Object Management Group (OMG), an open consortium of companies. The OMG was formed to build standards that supported interoperability, specifically the interoperability of object-oriented systems. The OMG is perhaps best known for the CORBA (Common Object Request Broker Architecture) standards.

The UML was born out of the unification of the many object-oriented graphical modeling languages that thrived in the late 1980s and early 1990s. Since its appearance in 1997, it has relegated that particular tower of Babel to history. That's a service I, and many other developers, am deeply thankful for.

1

Ways of Using the UML

At the heart of the role of the UML in software development are the different ways in which people want to use it, differences that carry over from other graphical modeling languages. These differences lead to long and difficult arguments about how the UML should be used.

To untangle this, Steve Mellor and I independently came up with a characterization of the three modes in which people use the UML: sketch, blueprint, and programming language. By far the most common of the three, at least to my biased eye, is **UML as sketch**. In this usage, developers use the UML to help communicate some aspects of a system. As with blueprints, you can use sketches in a forward-engineering or reverse-engineering direction. **Forward engineering** draws a UML diagram before you write code, while **reverse engineering** builds a UML diagram from existing code in order to help understand it.

The essence of sketching is selectivity. With forward sketching, you rough out some issues in code you are about to write, usually discussing them with a group of people on your team. Your aim is to use the sketches to help communicate ideas and alternatives about what you're about to do. You don't talk about all the code you are going to work on, only important issues that you want to run past your colleagues first or sections of the design that you want to visualize before you begin programming. Sessions like this can be very short: a 10-minute session to discuss a few hours of programming or a day to discuss a 2-week iteration.

With reverse engineering, you use sketches to explain how some part of a system works. You don't show every class, simply those that are interesting and worth talking about before you dig into the code.

Because sketching is pretty informal and dynamic, you need to do it quickly and collaboratively, so a common medium is a whiteboard. Sketches are also useful in documents, in which case the focus is communication rather than completeness. The tools used for sketching are lightweight drawing tools, and often people aren't too particular about keeping to every strict rule of the UML. Most UML diagrams shown in books, such as my other books, are sketches. Their emphasis is on selective communication rather than complete specification.

In contrast, **UML as blueprint** is about completeness. In forward engineering, the idea is that blueprints are developed by a designer whose job is to build a detailed design for a programmer to code up. That design should be sufficiently complete in that all design decisions are laid out, and the programmer should be able to follow it as a pretty straightforward activity that requires little thought. The designer may be the same person as the programmer, but usually the designer is a more senior developer who designs for a team of programmers. The inspiration for this approach is other forms of engineering in which professional engineers create engineering drawings that are handed over to construction companies to build.

Blueprinting may be used for all details, or a designer may draw blueprints to a particular area. A common approach is for a designer to develop blueprint-level models as far as interfaces of subsystems but then let developers work out the details of implementing those details.

In reverse engineering, blueprints aim to convey detailed information about the code either in paper documents or as an interactive graphical browser. The blueprints can show every detail about a class in a graphical form that's easier for developers to understand.

Blueprints require much more sophisticated tools than sketches do in order to handle the details required for the task. Specialized CASE (computer-aided software engineering) tools fall into this category, although the term CASE has become a dirty word, and vendors try to avoid it now. Forward-engineering tools support diagram drawing and back it up with a repository to hold the information. Reverse-engineering tools read source code and interpret from it into the repository and generate diagrams. Tools that can do both forward and reverse engineering like this are referred to as **round-trip** tools.

Some tools use the source code itself as the repository and use diagrams as a graphic viewport on the code. These tools tie much more closely into programming and often integrate directly with programming editors. I like to think of these as **tripless** tools.

The line between blueprints and sketches is somewhat blurry, but the distinction, I think, rests on the fact that sketches are deliberately incomplete, highlighting important information, while blueprints intend to be comprehensive, often with the aim of reducing programming to a simple and fairly mechanical activity. In a sound bite, I'd say that sketches are explorative, while blueprints are definitive.

As you do more and more in the UML and the programming gets increasingly mechanical, it becomes obvious that the programming should be automated. Indeed, many CASE tools do some form of code generation, which automates building a significant part of a system. Eventually, however, you reach the point at which all the system can be specified in the UML, and you reach **UML as programming language**. In this environment, developers draw UML diagrams that are compiled directly to executable code, and the UML becomes the source code. Obviously, this usage of UML demands particularly sophisticated tooling. (Also, the notions of forward and reverse engineering don't make any sense for this mode, as the UML and source code are the same thing.)

Model Driven Architecture and Executable UML

When people talk about the UML, they also often talk about **Model Driven Architecture (MDA)** [Kleppe et al.]. Essentially, MDA is a standard approach to using the UML as a programming language; the standard is controlled by the OMG, as is the UML. By producing a modeling environment that conforms to the MDA, vendors can create models that can also work with other MDA-compliant environments.

MDA is often talked about in the same breath as the UML because MDA uses the UML as its basic modeling language. But, of course, you don't have to be using MDA to use the UML.

MDA divides development work into two main areas. Modelers represent a particular application by creating a **Platform Independent Model (PIM)**. The PIM is a UML model that is independent of any particular technology. Tools can then turn a PIM into a **Platform Specific Model (PSM)**. The PSM is a model of a system targeted to a specific execution environment. Further tools then take the PSM and generate code for that platform. The PSM could be UML but doesn't have to be.

So if you want to build a warehousing system using MDA, you would start by creating a single PIM of your warehousing system. If you then wanted this warehousing system to run on J2EE and .NET, you would use some vendor tools to create two PSMs: one for each platform. Then further tools would generate code for the two platforms.

If the process of going from PIM to PSM to final code is completely automated, we have the UML as programming language. If any of the steps is manual, we have blueprints.

Steve Mellor has long been active in this kind of work and has recently used the term **Executable UML** [Mellor and Balcer]. Executable UML is similar to MDA but uses slightly different terms. Similarly, you begin with a platform-independent model that is equivalent to MDA's PIM. However, the next step is to use a Model Compiler to turn that UML model into a deployable system in a single step; hence, there's no need for the PSM. As the term *compiler* suggests, this step is completely automatic.

The model compilers are based on reusable archetypes. An **archetype** describes how to take an executable UML model and turn it into a particular programming platform. So for the warehousing example, you would buy a model compiler and two archetypes (J2EE and .NET). Run each archetype on your executable UML model, and you have your two versions of the warehousing system.

Executable UML does not use the full UML standard; many constructs of UML are considered to be unnecessary and are therefore not used. As a result, Executable UML is simpler than full UML.

All this sounds good, but how realistic is it? In my view, there are two issues here. First is the question of the tools: whether they are mature enough to do the job. This is something that changes over time; certainly, as I write this, they aren't widely used, and I haven't seen much of them in action.

A more fundamental issue is the whole notion of the UML as a programming language. In my view, it's worth using the UML as a programming language only if it results in something that's significantly more productive than using another programming language. I'm not convinced that it is, based on various graphical development environments I've worked with in the past. Even if it is more productive, it still needs to get a critical mass of users for it to make the mainstream. That's a big hurdle in itself. Like many old Smalltalkers, I consider Smalltalk to be much more productive than current mainstream languages. But as Smalltalk is now only a niche language, I don't see many projects using it. To avoid Smalltalk's fate, the UML has to be luckier, even if it is superior.

One of the interesting questions around the UML as programming language is how to model behavioral logic. UML 2 offers three ways of behavioral modeling: interaction diagrams, state diagrams, and activity diagrams. All have their proponents for programming in. If the UML does gain popularity as a programming language, it will be interesting to see which of these techniques become successful.

Another way in which people look at the UML is the range between using it for conceptual and for software modeling. Most people are familiar with the UML used for software modeling. In this **software perspective**, the elements of the UML map pretty directly to elements in a software system. As we shall see, the mapping is by no means prescriptive, but when we use the UML, we are talking about software elements.

With the **conceptual perspective**, the UML represents a description of the concepts of a domain of study. Here, we aren't talking about software elements so much as we are building a vocabulary to talk about a particular domain.

There are no hard-and-fast rules about perspective; as it turns out, there's really quite a large range of usage. Some tools automatically turn source code into the UML diagrams, treating the UML as an alternative view of the source.

That's very much a software perspective. If you use UML diagrams to try and understand the various meanings of the terms *asset pool* with a bunch of accountants, you are in a much more conceptual frame of mind.

In previous editions of this book, I split the software perspective into specification (interface) and implementation. In practice, I found that it was too hard to draw a precise line between the two, so I feel that the distinction is no longer worth making a fuss about. However, I'm always inclined to emphasize interface rather than implementation in my diagrams.

These different ways of using the UML lead to a host of arguments about what UML diagrams mean and what their relationship is to the rest of the world. In particular, it affects the relationship between the UML and source code. Some people hold the view that the UML should be used to create a design that is independent of the programming language that's used for implementation. Others believe that language-independent design is an oxymoron, with a strong emphasis on the moron.

Another difference in viewpoints is what the essence of the UML is. In my view, most users of the UML, particularly sketchers, see the essence of the UML to be the diagrams. However, the creators of the UML see the diagrams as secondary; the essence of the UML is the meta-model. Diagrams are simply a presentation of the meta-model. This view also makes sense to blueprinters and UML programming language users.

So whenever you read anything involving the UML, it's important to understand the point of view of the author. Only then can you make sense of the often fierce arguments that the UML encourages.

Having said all that, I need to make my biases clear. Almost all the time, my use of the UML is as sketches. I find the UML sketches useful with forward and reverse engineering and in both conceptual and software perspectives.

I'm not a fan of detailed forward-engineered blueprints; I believe that it's too difficult to do well and slows down a development effort. Blueprinting to a level of subsystem interfaces is reasonable, but even then you should expect to change those interfaces as developers implement the interactions across the interface. The value of reverse-engineered blueprints is dependent on how the tool works. If it's used as a dynamic browser, it can be very helpful; if it generates a large document, all it does is kill trees.

I see the UML as programming language as a nice idea but doubt that it will ever see significant usage. I'm not convinced that graphical forms are more productive than textual forms for most programming tasks and that even if they are, it's very difficult for a language to be widely accepted.

As a result of my biases, this book focuses much more on using the UML for sketching. Fortunately, this makes sense for a brief guide. I can't do justice to the UML in its other modes in a book this size, but a book this size makes a good introduction to other books that can. So if you're interested in the UML in its other modes, I'd suggest that you treat this book as an introduction and move on to other books as you need them. If you're interested only in sketches, this book may well be all you need.

How We Got to the UML

I'll admit, I'm a history buff. My favorite idea of light reading is a good history book. But I also know that it's not everybody's idea of fun. I talk about history here because I think that in many ways, it's hard to understand where the UML is without understanding the history of how it got here.

In the 1980s, objects began to move away from the research labs and took their first steps toward the "real" world. Smalltalk stabilized into a platform that people could use, and C++ was born. At that time, various people started thinking about object-oriented graphical design languages.

The key books about object-oriented graphical modeling languages appeared between 1988 and 1992. Leading figures included Grady Booch [Booch, OOAD]; Peter Coad [Coad, OOA], [Coad, OOD]; Ivar Jacobson (Objectory) [Jacobson, OOSE]; Jim Odell [Odell]; Jim Rumbaugh (OMT) [Rumbaugh, insights], [Rumbaugh, OMT]; Sally Shlaer and Steve Mellor [Shlaer and Mellor, data], [Shlaer and Mellor, states]; and Rebecca Wirfs-Brock (Responsibility Driven Design) [Wirfs-Brock].

Each of those authors was now informally leading a group of practitioners who liked those ideas. All these methods were very similar, yet they contained a number of often annoying minor differences among them. The same basic concepts would appear in very different notations, which caused confusion to my clients.

During that heady time, standardization was as talked about as it was ignored. A team from the OMG tried to look at standardization but got only an open letter of protest from all the key methodologists. (This reminds me of an old joke. Question: What is the difference between a methodologist and a terrorist? Answer: You can negotiate with a terrorist.)

The cataclysmic event that first initiated the UML was when Jim Rumbaugh left GE to join Grady Booch at Rational (now a part of IBM). The Booch/Rumbaugh alliance was seen from the beginning as one that could get a critical mass of market share. Grady and Jim proclaimed that "the methods war is over—we won," basically declaring that they were going to achieve standardization "the Microsoft way." A number of other methodologists suggested forming an Anti-Booch Coalition.

By OOPSLA '95, Grady and Jim had prepared their first public description of their merged method: version 0.8 of the *Unified Method* documentation. Even more significant, they announced that Rational Software had bought Objectory and that therefore, Ivar Jacobson would be joining the Unified team. Rational held a well-attended party to celebrate the release of the 0.8 draft. (The highlight of the party was the first public display of Jim Rumbaugh's singing; we all hope it's also the last.)

The next year saw a more open process emerge. The OMG, which had mostly stood on the sidelines, now took an active role. Rational had to incorporate Ivar's ideas and also spent time with other partners. More important, the OMG decided to take a major role.

At this point, it's important to realize why the OMG got involved. Methodologists, like book authors, like to think that they are important. But I don't think that the screams of book authors would even be heard by the OMG. What got the OMG involved were the screams of tools vendors, all of which were frightened that a standard controlled by Rational would give Rational tools an unfair competitive advantage. As a result, the vendors energized the OMG to do something about it, under the banner of CASE tool interoperability. This banner was important, as the OMG was all about interoperability. The idea was to create a UML that would allow CASE tools to freely exchange models.

Mary Loomis and Jim Odell chaired the initial task force. Odell made it clear that he was prepared to give up his method to a standard, but he did not want a Rational-imposed standard. In January 1997, various organizations submitted proposals for a methods standard to facilitate the interchange of models. Rational collaborated with a number of other organizations and released version 1.0 of the UML documentation as their proposal, the first animal to answer to the name Unified Modeling Language.

Then followed a short period of arm twisting while the various proposals were merged. The OMG adopted the resulting 1.1 as an official OMG standard. Some revisions were made later on. Revision 1.2 was entirely cosmetic. Revision 1.3 was more significant. Revision 1.4 added a number of detailed concepts around components and profiles. Revision 1.5 added action semantics.

When people talk about the UML, they credit mainly Grady Booch, Ivar Jacobson, and Jim Rumbaugh as its creators. They are generally referred to as the Three Amigos, although wags like to drop the first syllable of the second word. Although they are most credited with the UML, I think it somewhat unfair to give them the dominant credit. The UML notation was first formed in the Booch/Rumbaugh Unified Method. Since then, much of the work has been led by OMG committees. During these later stages, Jim Rumbaugh is the only one of the three to have made a heavy commitment. My view is that it's these members of the UML committee process that deserve the principal credit for the UML.

Notations and Meta-Models

The UML, in its current state, defines a notation and a meta-model. The **notation** is the graphical stuff you see in models; it is the graphical syntax of the modeling language. For instance, class diagram notation defines how items and concepts, such as class, association, and multiplicity, are represented.

Of course, this leads to the question of what exactly is meant by an association or multiplicity or even a class. Common usage suggests some informal definitions, but many people want more rigor than that.

The idea of rigorous specification and design languages is most prevalent in the field of formal methods. In such techniques, designs and specifications are represented using some derivative of predicate calculus. Such definitions are mathematically rigorous and allow no ambiguity. However, the value of these definitions is by no means universal. Even if you can prove that a program satisfies a mathematical specification, there is no way to prove that the mathematical specification meets the real requirements of the system.

Most graphical modeling languages have very little rigor; their notation appeals to intuition rather than to formal definition. On the whole, this does not seem to have done much harm. These methods may be informal, but many people still find them useful—and it is usefulness that counts.

However, methodologists are looking for ways to improve the rigor of methods without sacrificing their usefulness. One way to do this is to define a **meta-model:** a diagram, usually a class diagram, that defines the concepts of the language.

Figure 1.1, a small piece of the UML meta-model, shows the relationship among features. (The extract is there to give you a flavor of what meta-models are like. I'm not even going to try to explain it.)

How much does the meta-model affect a user of the modeling notation? The answer depends mostly on the mode of usage. A sketcher usually doesn't care too much; a blueprinter should care rather more. It's vitally important to those who use the UML as a programming language, as it defines the abstract syntax of that language.

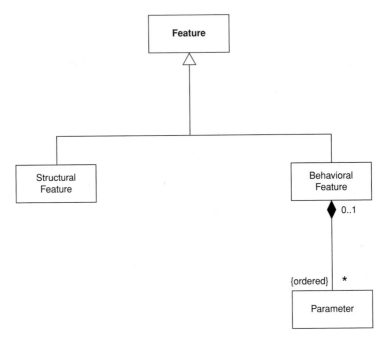

Figure 1.1 *A small piece of the UML meta-model*

Many of the people who are involved in the ongoing development of the UML are interested primarily in the meta-model, particularly as this is important to the usage of the UML as a programming language. Notational issues often run second place, which is important to bear in mind if you ever try to get familiar with the standards documents themselves.

As you get deeper into the more detailed usage of the UML, you realize that you need much more than the graphical notation. This is why UML tools are so complex.

I am not rigorous in this book. I prefer the traditional methods path and appeal mainly to your intuition. That's natural for a small book like this written by an author who's inclined mostly to a sketch usage. If you want more rigor, you should turn to more detailed tomes.

UML Diagrams

UML 2 describes 13 official diagram types listed in Table 1.1 and classified as indicated on Figure 1.2. Although these diagram types are the way many people

Table 1.1 *Official Diagram Types of the UML*

Diagram	Book Chapters	Purpose	Lineage
Activity	11	Procedural and parallel behavior	In UML 1
Class	3, 5	Class, features, and relationships	In UML 1
Communication	12	Interaction between objects; emphasis on links	UML 1 collaboration diagram
Component	14	Structure and connections of components	In UML 1
Composite structure	13	Runtime decomposition of a class	New to UML 2
Deployment	8	Deployment of artifacts to nodes	In UML 1
Interaction overview	16	Mix of sequence and activity diagram	New to UML 2
Object	6	Example configurations of instances	Unofficially in UML 1
Package	7	Compile-time hierarchic structure	Unofficially in UML 1
Sequence	4	Interaction between objects; emphasis on sequence	In UML 1
State machine	10	How events change an object over its life	In UML 1
Timing	17	Interaction between objects; emphasis on timing	New to UML 2
Use case	9	How users interact with a system	In UML 1

approach the UML and how I've organized this book, the UML's authors do not see diagrams as the central part of the UML. As a result, the diagram types are not particularly rigid. Often, you can legally use elements from one diagram type on another diagram. The UML standard indicates that certain elements are typically drawn on certain diagram types, but this is not a prescription.

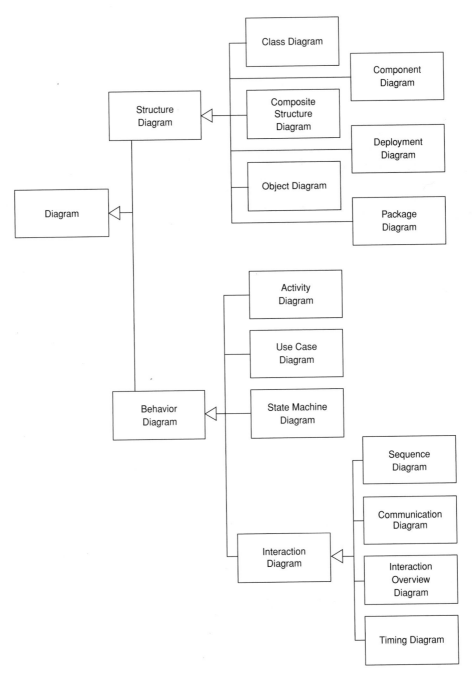

Figure 1.2 *Classification of UML diagram types*

What Is Legal UML?

At first blush, this should be a simple question to answer: Legal UML is what is defined as well formed in the specification. In practice, however, the answer is a bit more complicated.

An important part of this question is whether the UML has descriptive or prescriptive rules. A language with **prescriptive rules** is controlled by an official body that states what is or isn't legal in the language and what meaning you give to utterances in that language. A language with **descriptive rules** is one in which you understand its rules by looking at how people use the language in practice. Programming languages tend to have prescriptive rules set by a standards committee or dominant vendor, while natural languages, such as English, tend to have descriptive rules whose meaning is set by convention.

UML is quite a precise language, so you might expect it to have prescriptive rules. But UML is often considered to be the software equivalent of the blueprints in other engineering disciplines, and these blueprints are not prescriptive notations. No committee says what the legal symbols are on a structural engineering drawing; the notation has been accepted by convention, similarly to a natural language. Simply having a standards body doesn't do the trick either, because people in the field may not follow everything the standards body says; just ask the French about the Académie Française. In addition, the UML is so complex that the standard is often open to multiple interpretations. Even the UML leaders who reviewed this book would disagree on interpretation of the UML standard.

This issue is important both for me writing this book and for you using the UML. If you want to understand a UML diagram, it's important to realize that understanding the UML standard is not the whole picture. People do adopt conventions, both in the industry widely and within a particular project. As a result, although the UML standard can be the primary source of information on the UML, it can't be the only one.

My attitude is that, for most people, the UML has descriptive rules. The UML standard is the biggest single influence on what UML means, but it isn't the only one. I think that this will become particularly true with UML 2, which introduces some notational conventions that conflict with either UML 1's definition or the conventional usage of UML, as well as adds yet more complexity to the UML. In this book, therefore, I'm trying to summarize the UML as I find it: both the standards and the conventional usage. When I have to make a distinction in this book, I'll use the term **conventional use** to indicate something that isn't in the standard but that I think is widely used. For something that conforms to the standard, I'll use the terms **standard** or **normative**. (Normative is the term standards people use to mean a statement that you must conform to be valid in the standard. So non-normative UML is a fancy way of saying that something is strictly illegal according to the UML standard.)

When you are looking at a UML diagram, you should bear in mind that a general principle in the UML is that any information may be **suppressed** for a particular diagram. This suppression can occur either generally—hide all attributes—or specifically—don't show these three classes. In a diagram, therefore, you can never infer anything by its absence. If a multiplicity is missing, you cannot infer what value it might be. Even if the UML meta-model has a default, such as [1] for attributes, if you don't see the information on the diagram, it may be because it's the default or because it's suppressed.

Having said that, there are some general conventions, such as multivalued properties being sets. In the text, I'll point out these default conventions.

It's important to not put too much emphasis on having legal UML if you're a sketcher or blueprinter. It's more important to have a good design for your system, and I would rather have a good design in illegal UML than a legal but poor design. Obviously, good and legal is best, but you're better off putting your energy into having a good design than worrying about the arcana of UML. (Of course, you have to be legal in UML as programming language, or your program won't run properly!)

The Meaning of UML

One of the awkward issues about the UML is that, although the specification describes in great detail what well-formed UML is, it doesn't have much to say about what the UML means outside of the rarefied world of the UML meta-model. No formal definition exists of how the UML maps to any particular programming language. You cannot look at a UML diagram and say *exactly* what the equivalent code would look like. However, you can get a *rough idea* of what the code would look like. In practice, that's enough to be useful. Development teams often form their local conventions for these, and you'll need to be familiar with the ones in use.

UML Is Not Enough

Although the UML provides quite a considerable body of various diagrams that help to define an application, it's by no means a complete list of all the useful diagrams that you might want to use. In many places, different diagrams can be useful, and you shouldn't hesitate to use a non-UML diagram if no UML diagram suits your purpose.

Figure 1.3, a screen flow diagram, shows the various screens on a user interface and how you move between them. I've seen and used these screen flow diagrams for many years. I've never seen more than a very rough definition of what they mean; there isn't anything like it in the UML, yet I've found it a very useful diagram.

Table 1.2 shows another favorite: the decision table. Decision tables are a good way to show complicated logical conditions. You can do this with an activity diagram, but once you get beyond simple cases, the table is both more compact and more clear. Again, many forms of decision tables are out there. Table 1.2 divides the table into two sections: conditions above the double line and consequences below it. Each column shows how a particular combination of conditions leads to a particular set of consequences.

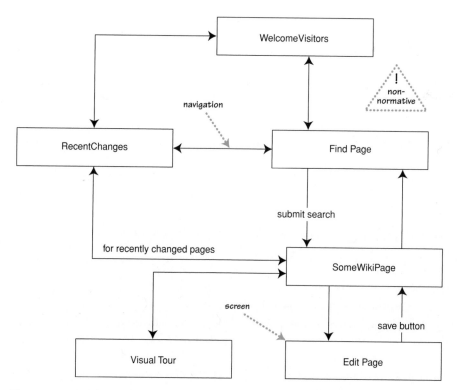

Figure 1.3 *An informal screen flow diagram for part of the wiki (http://c2.com/cgi/wiki)*

Table 1.2 *A Decision Table*

Premium customer	X	X	Y	Y	N	N
Priority order	Y	N	Y	N	Y	N
International order	Y	Y	N	N	N	N
Fee	$150	$100	$70	$50	$80	$60
Alert rep	•	•	•			

You'll run into various kinds of these things in various books. Don't hesitate to try out techniques that seem appropriate for your project. If they work well, use them. If not, discard them. (This is, of course, the same advice as for UML diagrams.)

Where to Start with the UML

Nobody, not even the creators of the UML, understand or use all of it. Most people use a small subset of the UML and work with that. You have to find the subset of the UML that works for you and your colleagues.

If you are starting out, I suggest that you concentrate first on the basic forms of class diagrams and sequence diagrams. These are the most common and, in my view, the most useful diagram types.

Once you've got the hang of those, you can start using some of the more advanced class diagram notation and take a look at the other diagrams types. Experiment with the diagrams and see how helpful they are to you. Don't be afraid to drop any that don't seem to be useful to your work.

Where to Find Out More

This book is not a complete and definitive reference to the UML, let alone OO analysis and design. A lot of words are out there and a lot of worthwhile things to read. As I discuss the individual topics, I also mention other books you should go to for more in-depth information there. Here are some general books on the UML and object-oriented design.

As with all book recommendations, you may need to check which version of the UML they are written for. As of June 2003, no published book uses UML 2.0, which is hardly surprising, as the ink is barely dry on the standard. The books I suggest are good books, but I can't tell whether or when they will be updated to the UML 2 standard.

If you are new to objects, I recommend my current favorite introductory book: [Larman]. The author's strong responsibility-driven approach to design is worth following.

For the conclusive word on the UML, you should look to the official standards documents; but remember, they are written for consenting methodologists in the privacy of their own cubicles. For a much more digestible version of the standard, take a look at [Rumbaugh, UML Reference].

For more detailed advice on object-oriented design, you'll learn many good things from [Martin].

I also suggest that you read books on patterns for material that will take you beyond the basics. Now that the methods war is over, patterns (page 27) are where most of the interesting material about analysis and design appears.

Chapter 2

Development Process

As I've already mentioned, the UML grew out of a bunch of OO analysis and design methods. To some extent, all of them mixed a graphical modeling language with a process that described how to go about developing software.

Interestingly, as the UML was formed, the various players discovered that although they could agree on a modeling language, they most certainly could not agree on a process. As a result, they agreed to leave any agreement on process until later and to confine the UML to being a modeling language.

The title of this book is *UML Distilled*, so I could have safely ignored process. However, I don't believe that modeling techniques make any sense without knowing how they fit into a process. The way you use the UML depends a lot on the style of process you use.

As a result, I think that it's important to talk about process first so that you can see the context for using the UML. I'm not going to go into great detail on any particular process; I simply want to give you enough information to see this context and pointers to where you can find out more.

When you hear people discuss the UML, you often hear them talk about the Rational Unified Process (RUP). RUP is one process—or, more strictly, a process framework—that you can use with the UML. But other than the common involvement of various people from Rational and the name "unified," it doesn't have any special relationship to the UML. The UML can be used with any process. RUP is a popular approach and is discussed on page 25.

Iterative and Waterfall Processes

One of the biggest debates about process is that between waterfall and iterative styles. The terms often get misused, particularly as iterative is seen as fashionable, while the waterfall process seems to wear plaid trousers. As a result, many projects claim to do iterative development but are really doing waterfall.

The essential difference between the two is how you break up a project into smaller chunks. If you have a project that you think will take a year, few people are comfortable telling the team to go away for a year and to come back when done. Some breakdown is needed so that people can approach the problem and track progress.

The **waterfall** style breaks down a project based on activity. To build software, you have to do certain activities: requirements analysis, design, coding, and testing. Our 1-year project might thus have a 2-month analysis phase, followed by a 4-month design phase, followed by a 3-month coding phase, followed by a 3-month testing phase.

The **iterative** style breaks down a project by subsets of functionality. You might take a year and break it into 3-month iterations. In the first iteration, you'd take a quarter of the requirements and do the complete software life cycle for that quarter: analysis, design, code, and test. At the end of the first iteration, you'd have a system that does a quarter of the needed functionality. Then you'd do a second iteration so that at the end of 6 months, you'd have a system that does half the functionality.

Of course, the above is a simplified description, but it is the essence of the difference. In practice, of course, some impurities leak into the process.

With waterfall development, there is usually some form of formal handoff between each phase, but there are often backflows. During coding, something may come up that causes you to revisit the analysis and design. You certainly should not assume that all design is finished when coding begins. It's inevitable that analysis and design decisions will have to be revisited in later phases. However, these backflows are exceptions and should be minimized as much as possible.

With iteration, you usually see some form of exploration activity before the true iterations begin. At the very least, this will get a high-level view of the requirements: at least enough to break the requirements down into the iterations that will follow. Some high-level design decisions may occur during exploration too. At the other end, although each iteration should produce production-ready integrated software, it often doesn't quite get to that point and needs a stabilization period to iron out the last bugs. Also, some activities, such as user training, are left to the end.

You may well not put the system into production at the end of each iteration, but the system should be of production quality. Often, however, you can put the system into production at regular intervals; this is good because you get value from the system earlier and you get better-quality feedback. In this situation, you often hear of a project having multiple **releases**, each of which is broken down into several **iterations**.

Iterative development has come under many names: incremental, spiral, evolutionary, and jacuzzi spring to mind. Various people make distinctions among them, but the distinctions are neither widely agreed on nor that important compared to the iterative/waterfall dichotomy.

You can have hybrid approaches. [McConnell] describes the **staged delivery** life cycle whereby analysis and high-level design are done first, in a waterfall style, and then the coding and testing are divided up into iterations. Such a project might have 4 months of analysis and design followed by four 2-month iterative builds of the system.

Most writers on software process in the past few years, especially in the object-oriented community, dislike the waterfall approach. Of the many reasons for this, the most fundamental is that it's very difficult to tell whether the project is truly on track with a waterfall process. It's too easy to declare victory with early phases and hide a schedule slip. Usually, the only way you can really tell whether you are on track is to produce tested, integrated software. By doing this repeatedly, an iterative style gives you better warning if something is going awry.

For that reason alone, I strongly recommend that projects do not use a pure waterfall approach. You should at least use staged delivery, if not a more pure iterative technique.

The OO community has long been in favor of iterative development, and it's safe to say that pretty much everyone involved in building the UML is in favor of at least some form of iterative development. My sense of industrial practice is that waterfall development is still the more common approach, however. One reason for this is what I refer to as pseudoiterative development: People claim to be doing iterative development but are in fact doing waterfall. Common symptoms of this are:

- "We are doing one analysis iteration followed by two design iterations. . . ."

- "This iteration's code is very buggy, but we'll clean it up at the end."

It is particularly important that each iteration produces tested, integrated code that is as close to production quality as possible. Testing and integration are the hardest activities to estimate, so it's important not to have an open-ended activity like that at the end of the project. The test should be that any iteration that's not scheduled to be released could be released without substantial extra development work.

A common technique with iterations is to use **time boxing**. This forces an iteration to be a fixed length of time. If it appears that you can't build all you intended to build during an iteration, you must decide to slip some functionality from the iteration; you must not slip the date of the iteration. Most projects that use iterative development use the same iteration length throughout the project; that way, you get a regular rhythm of builds.

I like time boxing because people usually have difficulty slipping functionality. By practicing slipping function regularly, they are in a better position to make an intelligent choice at a big release between slipping a date and slipping function. Slipping function during iterations is also effective at helping people learn what the real requirements priorities are.

One of the most common concerns about iterative development is the issue of rework. Iterative development explicitly assumes that you will be reworking and deleting existing code during the later iterations of a project. In many domains, such as manufacturing, rework is seen as a waste. But software isn't like manufacturing; as a result, it often is more efficient to rework existing code than to patch around code that was poorly designed. A number of technical practices can greatly help make rework be more efficient.

- **Automated regression tests** help by allowing you to quickly detect any defects that may have been introduced when you are changing things. The xUnit family of testing frameworks is a particularly valuable tool for building automated unit tests. Starting with the original JUnit **http://junit.org**, there are now ports to almost every language imaginable (see **http://www.xprogramming.com/software.htm**). A good rule of thumb is that the size of your unit test code should be about the same size as your production code.

- **Refactoring** is a disciplined technique for changing existing software [Fowler, refactoring]. Refactoring works by using a series of small behavior-preserving transformations to the code base. Many of these transformations can be automated (see **http://www.refactoring.com**).

- **Continuous integration** keeps a team in sync to avoid painful integration cycles [Fowler and Foemmel]. At the heart of this lies a fully automated build process that can be kicked off automatically whenever any member of the team checks code into the code base. Developers are expected to check in daily, so automated builds are done many times a day. The build process includes running a large block of automated regression tests so that any inconsistencies are caught quickly so they can be fixed easily.

All these technical practices have been popularized recently by Extreme Programming [Beck], although they were used before and can, and should, be used whether or not you use XP or any other agile process.

Predictive and Adaptive Planning

One reason that the waterfall endures is the desire for predictability in software development. Nothing is more frustrating than not having a clear idea how much it will cost to build some software and how long it will take to build it.

A predictive approach looks to do work early in the project in order to yield a greater understanding of what has to be done later. This way, you can reach a point where the latter part of the project can be estimated with a reasonable degree of accuracy. With **predictive planning**, a project has two stages. The first stage comes up with plans and is difficult to predict, but the second stage is much more predictable because the plans are in place.

This isn't necessarily a black-and-white affair. As the project goes on, you gradually get more predictability. And even once you have a predictive plan, things will go wrong. You simply expect that the deviations become less significant once a solid plan is in place.

However, there is a considerable debate about whether many software projects can ever be predictable. At the heart of this question is requirements analysis. One of the unique sources of complexity in software projects is the difficulty in understanding the requirements for a software system. The majority of software projects experience significant **requirements churn**: changes in requirements in the later stages of the project. These changes shatter the foundations of a predictive plan. You can combat these changes by freezing the requirements early on and not permitting changes, but this runs the risk of delivering a system that no longer meets the needs of its users.

This problem leads to two very different reactions. One route is to put more effort into the requirements process itself. This way, you may get a more accurate set of requirements, which will reduce the churn.

Another school contends that requirements churn is unavoidable, that it's too difficult for many projects to stabilize requirements sufficiently to use a predictive plan. This may be either owing to the sheer difficulty of envisioning what software can do or because market conditions force unpredictable changes. This school of thought advocates **adaptive planning,** whereby predictivity is seen as an illusion. Instead of fooling ourselves with illusory predictability, we should face the reality of constant change and use a planning approach that treats change as a constant in a software project. This change is controlled so that the project delivers the best software it can; but although the project is controllable, it is not predictable.

The difference between a predictive project and an adaptive project surfaces in many ways that people talk about how the project goes. When people talk about a project that's doing well because it's going according to plan, that's a predictive form of thinking. You can't say "according to plan" in an adaptive environment, because the plan is always changing. This doesn't mean that adaptive projects don't plan; they usually plan a lot, but the plan is treated as a baseline to assess the consequences of change rather than as a prediction of the future.

With a predictive plan, you can develop a fixed-price/fixed-scope contract. Such a contract says exactly what should be built, how much it will cost, and when it will be delivered. Such fixing isn't possible with an adaptive plan. You can fix a budget and a time for delivery, but you can't fix what functionality will be delivered. An adaptive contract assumes that the users will collaborate with the development team to regularly reassess what functionality needs to be built and will cancel the project if progress ends up being too slow. As such, an adaptive planning process can be fixed price/variable scope.

Naturally, the adaptive approach is less desirable, as anyone would prefer greater predictability in a software project. However, predictability depends on a precise, accurate, and stable set of requirements. If you cannot stabilize your requirements, the predictive plan is based on sand and the chances are high that the project goes off course. This leads to two important pieces of advice.

1. Don't make a predictive plan until you have precise and accurate requirements and are confident that they won't significantly change.

2. If you can't get precise, accurate, and stable requirements, use an adaptive planning style.

Predictivity and adaptivity feed into the choice of life cycle. An adaptive plan absolutely requires an iterative process. Predictive planning can be done either way, although it's easier to see how it works with waterfall or a staged delivery approach.

Agile Processes

In the past few years, there's been a lot of interest in agile software processes. *Agile* is an umbrella term that covers many processes that share a common set of values and principles as defined by the Manifesto of Agile Software Development (**http://agileManifesto.org**). Examples of these processes are Extreme Programming (XP), Scrum, Feature Driven Development (FDD), Crystal, and DSDM (Dynamic Systems Development Method).

In terms of our discussion, agile processes are strongly adaptive in their nature. They are also very much people-oriented processes. Agile approaches assume that the most important factor in a project's success is the quality of the people on the project and how well they work together in human terms. Which process they use and which tools they use are strictly second-order effects.

Agile methods tend to use short, time-boxed iterations, most often of a month or less. Because they don't attach much weight to documents, agile approaches disdain using the UML in blueprint mode. Most use the UML in sketch mode, with a few advocating using it as a programming language.

Agile processes tend to be low in **ceremony**. A high-ceremony, or heavyweight, process has a lot of documents and control points during the project. Agile processes consider that ceremony makes it harder to make changes and works against the grain of talented people. As a result, agile processes are often characterized as **lightweight**. It's important to realize that the lack of ceremony is a consequence of adaptivity and people orientation rather than a fundamental property.

Rational Unified Process

Although the Rational Unified Process (RUP) is independent of the UML, the two are often talked about together. So I think it's worth saying a few things about it here.

Although RUP is called a process, it actually is a process framework, providing a vocabulary and loose structure to talk about processes. When you use RUP, the first thing you need to do is choose a **development case**: the process you are going to use in the project. Development cases can vary widely, so don't assume that your development case will look that much like any other development case. Choosing a development case needs someone early on who is very familiar with RUP: someone who can tailor RUP for a particular project's needs. Alternatively, there is a growing body of packaged development cases to start from.

Whatever the development case, RUP is essentially an iterative process. A waterfall style isn't compatible with the philosophy of RUP, although sadly it's not uncommon to run into projects that use a waterfall-style process and dress it up in RUP's clothes.

All RUP projects should follow four phases.

1. **Inception** makes an initial evaluation of a project. Typically in inception, you decide whether to commit enough funds to do an elaboration phase.

2. **Elaboration** identifies the primary use cases of the project and builds software in iterations in order to shake out the architecture of the system. At

the end of elaboration, you should have a good sense of the requirements and a skeletal working system that acts as the seed of development. In particular, you should have found and resolved the major risks to the project.

3. **Construction** continues the building process, developing enough functionality to release.

4. **Transition** includes various late-stage activities that you don't do iteratively. These may include deployment into the data center, user training, and the like.

There's a fair amount of fuzziness between the phases, especially between elaboration and construction. For some, the shift to construction is the point at which you can move into a predictive planning mode. For others, it merely indicates the point at which you have a broad vision of requirements and an architecture that you think is going to last the rest of the project.

Sometimes, RUP is referred to as the Unified Process (UP). This is usually done by organizations that wish to use the terminology and overall style of RUP without using the licensed products of Rational Software. You can think of RUP as Rational's product offering based on the UP, or you can think of RUP and UP as the same thing. Either way, you'll find people who agree with you.

Fitting a Process to a Project

Software projects differ greatly from one another. The way you go about software development depends on many factors: the kind of system you're building, the technology you're using, the size and distribution of the team, the nature of the risks, the consequences of failure, the working styles of the team, and the culture of the organization. As a result, you should never expect there to be a one-size-fits-all process that will work for all projects.

Consequently, you always have to adapt a process to fit your particular environment. One of the first things you need to do is look at your project and consider which processes seem close to a fit. This should give you a short list of processes to consider.

You should then consider what adaptations you need to make to fit them to your project. You have to be somewhat careful with this. Many processes are difficult to fully appreciate until you've worked with them. In these cases, it's often worth using the process out of the box for a couple of iterations until you learn how it works. Then you can start modifying the process. If from the beginning you are more familiar with how a process works, you can modify it

Patterns

The UML tells you how to express an object-oriented design. Patterns look, instead, at the results of the process: example designs.

Many people have commented that projects have problems because the people involved were not aware of designs that are well known to those with more experience. Patterns describe common ways of doing things and are collected by people who spot repeating themes in designs. These people take each theme and describe it so that other people can read the pattern and see how to apply it.

Let's look at an example. Say that you have some objects running in a process on your desktop and that they need to communicate with other objects running in another process. Perhaps this process is also on your desktop; perhaps it resides elsewhere. You don't want the objects in your system to have to worry about finding other objects on the network or executing remote procedure calls.

What you can do is create a proxy object within your local process for the remote object. The proxy has the same interface as the remote object. Your local objects talk to the proxy, using the usual in-process message sends. The proxy then is responsible for passing any messages on to the real object, wherever it might reside.

Proxies are a common technique used in networks and elsewhere. People have a lot of experience using proxies, knowing how they can be used, what advantages they can bring, their limitations, and how to implement them. Methods books like this one don't discuss this knowledge; all they discuss is how you can diagram a proxy. Although this is useful, it is not as useful as discussing the experience involving proxies.

In the early 1990s, some people began to capture this experience. They formed a community interested in writing patterns. These people sponsor conferences and have produced several books.

The most famous patterns book to emerge from this group is [Gang of Four], which discusses 23 design patterns in detail. If you want to know about proxies, this book spends ten pages on the subject, giving details about how the objects work together, the benefits and limitations of the pattern, common variations, and implementation tips.

A pattern is much more than a model. A pattern must also include the reason why it is the way it is. It is often said that a pattern is a solution to a problem. The pattern must identify the problem clearly, explain why it solves the problem, and also explain the circumstances under which the pattern works and doesn't work.

Patterns are important because they are the next stage beyond understanding the basics of a language or a modeling technique. Patterns give you a series of solutions and also show you what makes a good model and how you go about constructing a model. Patterns teach by example.

When I started out, I wondered why I had to invent things from scratch. Why didn't I have handbooks to show me how to do common things? The patterns community is trying to build these handbooks.

There are now many patterns books out there, and they vary greatly in quality. My favorites are [Gang of Four], [POSA1], [POSA2], [Core J2EE Patterns], [Pont], and with suitable immodesty [Fowler, AP] and [Fowler, P of EAA]. You can also take a look at the patterns home page: **http://www.hillside.net/patterns.**

from the beginning. Remember that it's usually easier to start with too little and add things than it is to start with too much and take things away.

However confident you are with your process when you begin, it's essential to learn as you go along. Indeed, one of the great benefits of iterative development is that it supports frequent process improvement.

At the end of each iteration, conduct an **iteration retrospective**, whereby the team assembles to consider how things went and how they can be improved. A couple of hours is plenty if your iterations are short. A good way to do this is to make a list with three categories:

1. *Keep:* things that worked well that you want to ensure you continue to do

2. *Problems:* areas that aren't working well

3. *Try:* changes to your process to improve it

You can start each iteration retrospective after the first by reviewing the items from the previous session and seeing how things have changed. Don't forget the list of things to keep; it's important to keep track of things that are working. If you don't do that, you can lose a sense of perspective on the project and potentially stop paying attention to winning practices.

At the end of a project or at a major release, you may want to consider a more formal **project retrospective** that will last a couple of days; see **http://www.retrospectives.com/** and [Kerth] for more details. One of my biggest irritations is how organizations consistently fail to learn from their own experience and end up making expensive mistakes time and time again.

Fitting the UML into a Process

When they look at graphical modeling languages, people usually think of them in the context of a waterfall process. A waterfall process usually has documents that act as the handoffs between analysis, design, and coding phases. Graphical models can often form a major part of these documents. Indeed, many of the structured methods from the 1970s and 1980s talk a lot about analysis and design models like this.

Whether or not you use a waterfall approach, you still do the activities of analysis, design, coding, and testing. You can run an iterative project with 1-week iterations, with each week a miniwaterfall.

Using the UML doesn't necessarily imply developing documents or feeding a complex CASE tool. Many people draw UML diagrams on whiteboards only during a meeting to help communicate their ideas.

Requirements Analysis

The activity of requirements analysis involves trying to figure out what the users and customers of a software effort want the system to do. A number of UML techniques can come in handy here:

- Use cases, which describe how people interact with the system.

- A class diagram drawn from the conceptual perspective, which can be a good way of building up a rigorous vocabulary of the domain.

- An activity diagram, which can show the work flow of the organization, showing how software and human activities interact. An activity diagram can show the context for use cases and also the details of how a complicated use case works.

- A state diagram, which can be useful if a concept has an interesting life cycle, with various states and events that change that state.

When working in requirements analysis, remember that the most important thing is communication with your users and customers. Usually, they are not software people and will be unfamiliar with the UML or any other technique.

Even so, I've had success using these techniques with nontechnical people. To do this, remember that it's important to keep the notation to a minimum. Don't introduce anything that is specific to the software implementation.

Be prepared to break the rules of the UML at any time if it helps you communicate better. The biggest risk with using the UML in analysis is that you draw diagrams that the domain experts don't fully understand. A diagram that isn't understood by the people who know the domain is worse than useless; all it does is breed a false sense of confidence for the development team.

Design

When you are doing design, you can get more technical with your diagrams. You can use more notation and be more precise about your notation. Some useful techniques are

- Class diagrams from a software perspective. These show the classes in the software and how they interrelate.

- Sequence diagrams for common scenarios. A valuable approach is to pick the most important and interesting scenarios from the use cases and use CRC cards or sequence diagrams to figure out what happens in the software.

- Package diagrams to show the large-scale organization of the software.

- State diagrams for classes with complex life histories.

- Deployment diagrams to show the physical layout of the software.

Many of these same techniques can be used to document software once it's been written. This may help people find their way around the software if they have to work on it and are not familiar with the code.

With a waterfall life cycle, you would do these diagrams and activities as part of the phases. The end-of-phase documents usually include the appropriate UML diagrams for that activity. A waterfall style usually implies that the UML is used as a blueprint.

In an iterative style, the UML diagrams can be used in either a blueprint or a sketch style. With a blueprint, the analysis diagrams will usually be built in the iteration prior to the one that builds the functionality. Each iteration doesn't start from scratch; rather, it modifies the existing body of documents, highlighting the changes in the new iteration.

Blueprint designs are usually done early in the iteration and may be done in pieces for different bits of functionality that are targeted for the iteration.

Again, iteration implies making changes to an existing model rather than building a new model each time.

Using the UML in sketch mode implies a more fluid process. One approach is to spend a couple of days at the beginning of an iteration, sketching out the design for that iteration. You can also do short design sessions at any point during the iteration, setting up a quick meeting for half an hour whenever a developer starts to tackle a nontrivial function.

With a blueprint, you expect the code implementation to follow the diagrams. A change from the blueprint is a deviation that needs review from the designers who did the blueprint. A sketch is usually treated more as a first cut at the design; if, during coding, people find that the sketch isn't exactly right, they should feel free to change the design. The implementors have to use their judgment as to whether the change needs a wider discussion to understand the full ramifications.

One of my concerns with blueprints is my own observation that it's very hard to get them right, even for a good designer. I often find that my own designs do not survive contact with coding intact. I still find UML sketches useful, but I don't find that they can be treated as absolutes.

In both modes, it makes sense to explore a number of design alternatives. It's usually best to explore alternatives in sketch mode so that you can quickly generate and change the alternatives. Once you pick a design to run with, you can either use that sketch or detail it into a blueprint.

Documentation

Once you have built the software, you can use the UML to help document what you have done. For this, I find UML diagrams useful for getting an overall understanding of a system. In doing this, however, I should stress that I do not believe in producing detailed diagrams of the whole system. To quote Ward Cunningham [Cunningham]:

> *Carefully selected and well-written memos can easily substitute for traditional comprehensive design documentation. The latter rarely shines except in isolated spots. Elevate those spots . . . and forget about the rest.*
> *(p. 384)*

I believe that detailed documentation should be generated from the code—like, for instance, JavaDoc. You should write additional documentation to highlight important concepts. Think of these as comprising a first step for the reader before he or she goes into the code-based details. I like to structure these as prose documents, short enough to read over a cup of coffee, using UML diagrams to help illustrate the discussion. I prefer the diagrams as sketches that highlight the most important parts of the system. Obviously, the writer of the document needs to decide what is important and what isn't, but the writer is much better equipped than the reader to do that.

A package diagram makes a good logical road map of the system. This diagram helps me understand the logical pieces of the system and see the dependencies and keep them under control. A deployment diagram (see Chapter 8), which shows the high-level physical picture, may also prove useful at this stage.

Within each package, I like to see a class diagram. I don't show every operation on every class. I show only the important features that help me understand what is in there. This class diagram acts as a graphical table of contents.

The class diagram should be supported by a handful of interaction diagrams that show the most important interactions in the system. Again, selectivity is important here; remember that, in this kind of document, comprehensiveness is the enemy of comprehensibility.

If a class has complex life-cycle behavior, I draw a state machine diagram (see Chapter 10) to describe it. I do this only if the behavior is sufficiently complex, which I find doesn't happen often.

I'll often include some important code, written in a literate program style. If a particularly complex algorithm is involved, I'll consider using an activity diagram (see Chapter 11) but only if it gives me more understanding than the code alone.

If I find concepts that are coming up repeatedly, I use patterns (page 27) to capture the basic ideas.

One of the most important things to document is the design alternatives you didn't take and why you didn't do them. That's often the most forgotten but most useful piece of external documentation you can provide.

Understanding Legacy Code

The UML can help you figure out a gnarly bunch of unfamiliar code in a couple of ways. Building a sketch of key facts can act as a graphical note-taking mechanism that helps you capture important information as you learn about it. Sketches of key classes in a package and their key interactions can help clarify what's going on.

With modern tools, you can generate detailed diagrams for key parts of a system. Don't use these tools to generate big paper reports; instead, use them to drill into key areas as you are exploring the code itself. A particularly nice capability is that of generating a sequence diagram to see how multiple objects collaborate in handling a complex method.

Choosing a Development Process

I'm strongly in favor of iterative development processes. As I've said in this book before: You should use iterative development only on projects that you want to succeed.

Perhaps that's a bit glib, but as I get older, I get more aggressive about using iterative development. Done well, it is an essential technique, one you can use to expose risk early and to obtain better control over development. It is not the same as having no management, although to be fair, I should point out that some have used it that way. It does need to be well planned. But it is a solid approach, and every OO development book encourages using it—for good reason.

You should not be surprised to hear that as one the authors of the Manifesto for Agile Software Development, I'm very much a fan of agile approaches. I've also had a lot of positive experiences with Extreme Programming, and certainly you should consider its practices very seriously.

Where to Find Out More

Books on software process have always been common, and the rise of agile software development has led to many new books. Overall, my favorite book on process in general is [McConnell]. He gives a broad and practical coverage of many of the issues involved in software development and a long list of useful practices.

From the agile community, [Cockburn, agile] and [Highsmith] provide a good overview. For a lot of good advice about applying the UML in an agile way, see [Ambler].

One of the most popular agile methods is Extreme Programming (XP), which you can delve into via such Web sites as **http://xprogramming.com** and **http://www.extremeprogramming.org**. XP has spawned many books, which is why I now refer to it as the formerly lightweight methodology. The usual starting point is [Beck].

Although it's written for XP, [Beck and Fowler] gives more details on planning an iterative project. Much of this is also covered by the other XP books, but if you're interested only in the planning aspect, this would be a good choice.

For more information on the Rational Unified Process, my favorite introduction is [Kruchten].

Chapter 3

Class Diagrams:
The Essentials

If someone were to come up to you in a dark alley and say, "Psst, wanna see a UML diagram?" that diagram would probably be a class diagram. The majority of UML diagrams I see are class diagrams.

The class diagram is not only widely used but also subject to the greatest range of modeling concepts. Although the basic elements are needed by everyone, the advanced concepts are used less often. Therefore, I've broken my discussion of class diagrams into two parts: the essentials (this chapter) and the advanced (Chapter 5).

A **class diagram** describes the types of objects in the system and the various kinds of static relationships that exist among them. Class diagrams also show the properties and operations of a class and the constraints that apply to the way objects are connected. The UML uses the term **feature** as a general term that covers properties and operations of a class.

Figure 3.1 shows a simple class model that would not surprise anyone who has worked with order processing. The boxes in the diagram are classes, which are divided into three compartments: the name of the class (in bold), its attributes, and its operations. Figure 3.1 also shows two kinds of relationships between classes: associations and generalizations.

Properties

Properties represent structural features of a class. As a first approximation, you can think of properties as corresponding to fields in a class. The reality is rather involved, as we shall see, but that's a reasonable place to start.

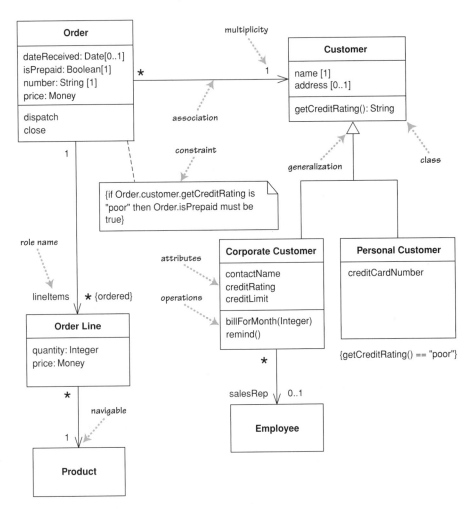

Figure 3.1 *A simple class diagram*

Properties are a single concept, but they appear in two quite distinct notations: attributes and associations. Although they look quite different on a diagram, they are really the same thing.

Attributes

The **attribute** notation describes a property as a line of text within the class box itself. The full form of an attribute is:

```
visibility name: type multiplicity = default {property-string}
```

An example of this is:

`- name: String [1] = "Untitled" {readOnly}`

Only the `name` is necessary.

- This `visibility` marker indicates whether the attribute is public (+) or private (-); I'll discuss other visibilities on page 83.

- The `name` of the attribute—how the class refers to the attribute—roughly corresponds to the name of a field in a programming language.

- The `type` of the attribute indicates a restriction on what kind of object may be placed in the attribute. You can think of this as the type of a field in a programming language.

- I'll explain `multiplicity` on page 38.

- The `default` value is the value for a newly created object if the attribute isn't specified during creation.

- The `{property-string}` allows you to indicate additional properties for the attribute. In the example, I used `{readOnly}` to indicate that clients may not modify the property. If this is missing, you can usually assume that the attribute is modifiable. I'll describe other property strings as we go.

Associations

The other way to notate a property is as an association. Much of the same information that you can show on an attribute appears on an association. Figures 3.2 and 3.3 show the same properties represented in the two different notations.

An **association** is a solid line between two classes, directed from the source class to the target class. The name of the property goes at the target end of the

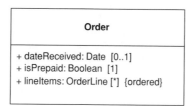

Figure 3.2 *Showing properties of an order as attributes*

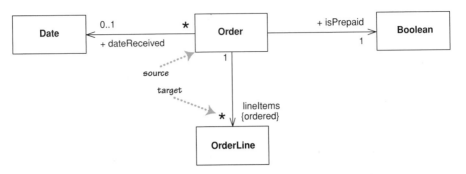

Figure 3.3 *Showing properties of an order as associations*

association, together with its multiplicity. The target end of the association links to the class that is the type of the property.

Although most of the same information appears in both notations, some items are different. In particular, associations can show multiplicities at both ends of the line.

With two notations for the same thing, the obvious question is, Why should you use one or the other? In general, I tend to use attributes for small things, such as dates or Booleans—in general, value types (page 73)—and associations for more significant classes, such as customers and orders. I also tend to prefer to use class boxes for classes that are significant for the diagram, which leads to using associations, and attributes for things less important for that diagram. The choice is much more about emphasis than about any underlying meaning.

Multiplicity

The **multiplicity** of a property is an indication of how many objects may fill the property. The most common multiplicities you will see are

- **1** (An order must have exactly one customer.)

- **0..1** (A corporate customer may or may not have a single sales rep.)

- ***** (A customer need not place an Order and there is no upper limit to the number of Orders a Customer may place—zero or more orders.)

More generally, multiplicities are defined with a lower bound and an upper bound, such as 2..4 for players of a game of canasta. The lower bound may be any positive number or zero; the upper is any positive number or * (for unlimited). If the lower and upper bounds are the same, you can use one number; hence, 1 is equivalent to 1..1. Because it's a common case, * is short for 0..*.

In attributes, you come across various terms that refer to the multiplicity.

- **Optional** implies a lower bound of 0.

- **Mandatory** implies a lower bound of 1 or possibly more.

- **Single-valued** implies an upper bound of 1.

- **Multivalued** implies an upper bound of more than 1: usually *.

If I have a multivalued property, I prefer to use a plural form for its name.

By default, the elements in a multivalued multiplicity form a set, so if you ask a customer for its orders, they do not come back in any order. If the ordering of the orders in association has meaning, you need to add {ordered} to the association end. If you want to allow duplicates, add {nonunique}. (If you want to explicitly show the default, you can use {unordered} and {unique}.) You may also see collection-oriented names, such as {bag} for unordered, nonunique.

UML 1 allowed discontinuous multiplicities, such as 2, 4 (meaning 2 or 4, as in cars in the days before minivans). Discontinuous multiplicities weren't very common and UML 2 removed them.

The default multiplicity of an attribute is [1]. Although this is true in the meta-model, you can't assume that an attribute in a diagram that's missing a multiplicity has a value of [1], as the diagram may be suppressing the multiplicity information. As a result, I prefer to explicitly state a [1] multiplicity if it's important.

Programming Interpretation of Properties

As with anything else in the UML, there's no one way to interpret properties in code. The most common software representation is that of a field or property of your programming language. So the Order Line class from Figure 3.1 would correspond to something like the following in Java:

```
public class OrderLine...
   private int quantity;
   private Money price;
   private Order order;
   private Product product
```

In a language like C#, which has properties, it would correspond to:

```
public class OrderLine ...
  public int Quantity;
  public Money Price;
  public Order Order;
  public Product Product;
```

Note that an attribute typically corresponds to public properties in a language that supports properties but to private fields in a language that does not. In a language without properties, you may see the fields exposed through accessor (getting and setting) methods. A read-only attribute will have no setting method (with fields) or set action (for properties). Note that if you don't give a name for a property, it's common to use the name of the target class.

Using private fields is a very implementation-focused interpretation of the diagram. A more interface-oriented interpretation might instead concentrate on the getting methods rather than the underlying data. In this case, we might see the Order Line's attributes corresponding to the following methods:

```
public class OrderLine...
  private int quantity;
  private Product product;
  public int getQuantity() {
    return quantity;
  }
  public void setQuantity(int quantity) {
    this.quantity = quantity;
  }
  public Money getPrice() {
    return product.getPrice().multiply(quantity);
  }
```

In this case, there is no data field for price; instead, it's a computed value. But as far as clients of the Order Line class are concerned, it looks the same as a field. Clients can't tell what is a field and what is computed. This information hiding is the essence of encapsulation.

If an attribute is multivalued, this implies that the data concerned is a collection. So an Order class would refer to a collection of Order Lines. Because this multiplicity is ordered, that collection must be ordered, (such as a List in Java or an IList in .NET). If the collection is unordered, it should, strictly, have no meaningful order and thus be implemented with a set, but most people implement unordered attributes as lists as well. Some people use arrays, but the UML implies an unlimited upper bound, so I almost always use a collection for data structure.

Multivalued properties yield a different kind of interface to single-valued properties (in Java):

```
class Order {
  private Set lineItems = new HashSet();
  public Set getLineItems() {
    return Collections.unmodifiableSet(lineItems);
  }
  public void addLineItem (OrderItem arg) {
    lineItems.add (arg);
  }
  public void removeLineItem (OrderItem arg) {
    lineItems.remove(arg);
  }
```

In most cases, you don't assign to a multivalued property; instead, you update with add and remove methods. In order to control its Line Items property, the order must control membership of that collection; as a result, it shouldn't pass out the naked collection. In this case, I used a protection proxy to provide a read-only wrapper to the collection. You can also provide a nonupdatable iterator or make a copy. It's okay for clients to modify the member objects, but the clients shouldn't directly change the collection itself.

Because multivalued attributes imply collections, you almost never see collection classes on a class diagram. You would show them only in very low level implementation diagrams of collections themselves.

You should be very afraid of classes that are nothing but a collection of fields and their accessors. Object-oriented design is about providing objects that are able to do rich behavior, so they shouldn't be simply providing data to other objects. If you are making repeated calls for data by using accessors, that's a sign that some behavior should be moved to the object that has the data.

These examples also reinforce the fact that there is no hard-and-fast correspondence between the UML and code, yet there is a similarity. Within a project team, team conventions will lead to a closer correspondence.

Whether a property is implemented as a field or as a calculated value, it represents something an object can always provide. You shouldn't use a property to model a transient relationship, such as an object that is passed as a parameter during a method call and used only within the confines of that interaction.

Bidirectional Associations

The associations we've looked at so far are called unidirectional associations. Another common kind of association is a bidirectional association, such as Figure 3.4.

Figure 3.4 *A bidirectional association*

A bidirectional association is a pair of properties that are linked together as inverses. The Car class has property `owner:Person[0..1]`, and the Person class has a property `cars:Car[*]`. (Note how I named the cars property in the plural form of the property's type, a common but non-normative convention.)

The inverse link between them implies that if you follow both properties, you should get back to a set that contains your starting point. For example, if I begin with a particular MG Midget, find its owner, and then look at its owner's cars, that set should contain the Midget that I started from.

As an alternative to labeling an association by a property, many people, particularly if they have a data-modeling background, like to label an association by using a verb phrase (Figure 3.5) so that the relationship can be used in a sentence. This is legal and you can add an arrow to the association to avoid ambiguity. Most object modelers prefer to use a property name, as that corresponds better to responsibilities and operations.

Some people name every association in some way. I choose to name an association only when doing so improves understanding. I've seen too many associations with such names as "has" or "is related to."

In Figure 3.4, the bidirectional nature of the association is made obvious by the **navigability arrows** at both ends of the association. Figure 3.5 has no arrows; the UML allows you to use this form either to indicate a bidirectional association or when you aren't showing navigability. My preference is to use the double-headed arrow of Figure 3.4 when you want to make it clear that you have a bidirectional association.

Implementing a bidirectional association in a programming language is often a little tricky because you have to be sure that both properties are kept

Figure 3.5 *Using a verb phrase to name an association*

synchronized. Using C#, I use code along these lines to implement a bidirectional association:

```
class Car...
  public Person Owner {
    get {return _owner;}
    set {
      if (_owner != null) _owner.friendCars().Remove(this);
      _owner = value;
      if (_owner != null) _owner.friendCars().Add(this);
    }
  }
  private Person _owner;
...

class Person ...
  public IList Cars {
    get {return ArrayList.ReadOnly(_cars);}
  }
  public void AddCar(Car arg) {
    arg.Owner = this;
  }
  private IList _cars = new ArrayList();
  internal IList friendCars() {
    //should only be used by Car.Owner
    return _cars;
  }
....
```

The primary thing is to let one side of the association—a single-valued side, if possible—control the relationship. For this to work, the slave end (Person) needs to leak the encapsulation of its data to the master end. This adds to the slave class an awkward method, which shouldn't really be there, unless the language has fine-grained access control. I've used the naming convention of "friend" here as a nod to C++, where the master's setter would indeed be a friend. Like much property code, this is pretty boilerplate stuff, which is why many people prefer to use some form of code generation to produce it.

In conceptual models, navigability isn't an important issue, so I don't show any navigability arrows on conceptual models.

Operations

Operations are the actions that a class knows to carry out. Operations most obviously correspond to the methods on a class. Normally, you don't show those operations that simply manipulate properties, because they can usually be inferred.

The full UML syntax for operations is:

```
visibility name (parameter-list) : return-type {property-string}
```

- This `visibility` marker is public (+) or private (-); others on page 83.

- The `name` is a string.

- The `parameter-list` is the list of parameters for the operation.

- The `return-type` is the type of the returned value, if there is one.

- The `property-string` indicates property values that apply to the given operation.

The parameters in the parameter list are notated in a similar way to attributes. The form is:

```
direction name: type = default value
```

- The `name`, `type`, and `default value` are the same as for attributes.

- The `direction` indicates whether the parameter is input (`in`), output (`out`) or both (`inout`). If no direction is shown, it's assumed to be `in`.

An example operation on account might be:

```
+ balanceOn (date: Date) : Money
```

With conceptual models, you shouldn't use operations to specify the interface of a class. Instead, use them to indicate the principal responsibilities of that class, perhaps using a couple of words summarizing a CRC responsibility (page 65).

I often find it useful to distinguish between operations that change the state of the system and those that don't. UML defines a **query** as an operation that gets a value from a class without changing the system state—in other words, without side effects. You can mark such an operation with the property string {query}. I refer to operations that do change state as **modifiers,** also called commands.

Strictly, the difference between query and modifiers is whether they change the observable state [Meyer]. The observable state is what can be perceived from the outside. An operation that updates a cache would alter the internal state but would have no effect that's observable from the outside.

I find it helpful to highlight queries, as you can change the order of execution of queries and not change the system behavior. A common convention is to try to write operations so that modifiers do not return a value; that way, you can rely on the fact that operations that return a value are queries. [Meyer] refers to this as the Command-Query separation principle. It's sometimes awkward to do this all the time, but you should do it as much as you can.

Other terms you sometimes see are getting methods and setting methods. A **getting method** returns a value from a field (and does nothing else). A **setting method** puts a value into a field (and does nothing else). From the outside, a client should not be able to tell whether a query is a getting method or a modifier is a setting method. Knowledge of getting and setting methods is entirely internal to the class.

Another distinction is between operation and method. An **operation** is something that is invoked on an object—the procedure declaration—whereas a **method** is the body of a procedure. The two are different when you have polymorphism. If you have a supertype with three subtypes, each of which overrides the supertype's getPrice operation, you have one operation and four methods that implement it.

People usually use the terms *operation* and *method* interchangeably, but there are times when it is useful to be precise about the difference.

Generalization

A typical example of **generalization** involves the personal and corporate customers of a business. They have differences but also many similarities. The similarities can be placed in a general Customer class (the supertype), with Personal Customer and Corporate Customer as subtypes.

This phenomenon is also subject to various interpretations at the various perspectives of modeling. Conceptually, we can say that Corporate Customer is a subtype of Customer if all instances of Corporate Customer are also, by definition, instances of Customer. A Corporate Customer is then a special kind of Customer. The key idea is that everything we say about a Customer—associations, attributes, operations—is true also for a Corporate Customer.

With a software perspective, the obvious interpretation is inheritance: The Corporate Customer is a subclass of Customer. In mainstream OO languages, the subclass inherits all the features of the superclass and may override any superclass methods.

An important principle of using inheritance effectively is **substitutability**. I should be able to substitute a Corporate Customer within any code that requires a Customer, and everything should work fine. Essentially, this means that if I write code assuming I have a Customer, I can freely use any subtype of Customer. The Corporate Customer may respond to certain commands differently from another Customer, using polymorphism, but the caller should not need to worry about the difference. (For more on this, see the Liskov Substitution Principle (LSP) in [Martin].)

Although inheritance is a powerful mechanism, it brings in a lot of baggage that isn't always needed to achieve substitutability. A good example of this was in the early days of Java, when many people didn't like the implementation of the built-in Vector class and wanted to replace it with something lighter. However, the only way they could produce a class that was substitutable for Vector was to subclass it, and that meant inheriting a lot of unwanted data and behavior.

Many other mechanisms can be used to provide substitutable classes. As a result, many people like to differentiate between subtyping, or interface inheritance, and subclassing, or implementation inheritance. A class is a **subtype** if it is substitutable for its supertype, whether or not it uses inheritance. **Subclassing** is used as a synonym for regular inheritance.

Many other mechanisms are available that allow you to have subtyping without subclassing. Examples are implementing an interface (page 69) and many of the standard design patterns [Gang of Four].

Notes and Comments

Notes are comments in the diagrams. Notes can stand on their own, or they can be linked with a dashed line to the elements they are commenting (Figure 3.6). They can appear in any kind of diagram.

The dashed line can sometimes be awkward because you can't position exactly where this line ends. So a common convention is to put a very small open circle at the end of the line. Sometimes, it's useful to have an in-line comment on a diagram element. You can do this by prefixing the text with two dashes: --.

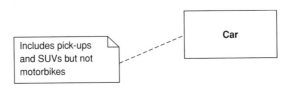

Figure 3.6 *A note is used as a comment on one or more diagram elements*

Dependency

A **dependency** exists between two elements if changes to the definition of one element (the **supplier** or target) may cause changes to the other (the **client** or source). With classes, dependencies exist for various reasons: One class sends a message to another; one class has another as part of its data; one class mentions another as a parameter to an operation. If a class changes its interface, any message sent to that class may no longer be valid.

As computer systems grow, you have to worry more and more about controlling dependencies. If dependencies get out of control, each change to a system has a wide ripple effect as more and more things have to change. The bigger the ripple, the harder it is to change anything.

The UML allows you to depict dependencies between all sorts of elements. You use dependencies whenever you want to show how changes in one element might alter other elements.

Figure 3.7 shows some dependencies that you might find in a multilayered application. The Benefits Window class—a user interface, or **presentation** class— is dependent on the Employee class: a **domain object** that captures the essential behavior of the system—in this case, business rules. This means that if the employee class changes its interface, the Benefits Window may have to change.

The important thing here is that the dependency is in only one direction and goes from the presentation class to the domain class. This way, we know that we can freely alter the Benefits Window without those changes having any effect on the Employee or other domain objects. I've found that a strict separation of presentation and domain logic, with the presentation depending on the domain but not vice versa, has been a valuable rule for me to follow.

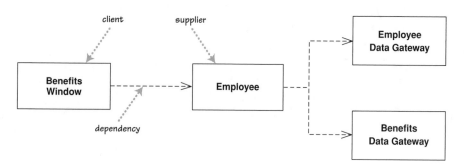

Figure 3.7 *Example dependencies*

A second notable thing from this diagram is that there is no direct dependency from the Benefits Window to the two Data Gateway classes. If these classes change, the Employee class may have to change. But if the change is only to the implementation of the Employee class, not its interface, the change stops there.

The UML has many varieties of dependency, each with particular semantics and keywords. The basic dependency that I've outlined here is the one I find the most useful, and I usually use it without keywords. To add more detail, you can add an appropriate keyword (Table 3.1).

The basic dependency is not a transitive relationship. An example of a **transitive** relationship is the "larger beard" relationship. If Jim has a larger beard than Grady, and Grady has a larger beard than Ivar, we can deduce that Jim has a larger beard than Ivar. Some kind of dependencies, such as substitute, are transitive, but in most cases there is a significant difference between direct and indirect dependencies, as there is in Figure 3.7.

Many UML relationships imply a dependency. The navigable association from Order to Customer in Figure 3.1 means that Order is dependent on Customer. A subclass is dependent on its superclass but not vice versa.

Table 3.1 *Selected Dependency Keywords*

Keyword	Meaning
«call»	The source calls an operation in the target.
«create»	The source creates instances of the target.
«derive»	The source is derived from the target.
«instantiate»	The source is an instance of the target. (Note that if the source is a class, the class itself is an instance of the class class; that is, the target class is a metaclass).
«permit»	The target allows the source to access the target's private features.
«realize»	The source is an implementation of a specification or interface defined by the target (page 69).
«refine»	Refinement indicates a relationship between different semantic levels; for example, the source might be a design class and the target the corresponding analysis class.
«substitute»	The source is substitutable for the target (page 45).
«trace»	Used to track such things as requirements to classes or how changes in one model link to changes elsewhere.
«use»	The source requires the target for its implementation.

Your general rule should be to minimize dependencies, particularly when they cross large areas of a system. In particular, you should be wary of cycles, as they can lead to a cycle of changes. I'm not super strict on this. I don't mind mutual dependencies between closely related classes, but I do try to eliminate cycles at a broader level, particularly between packages.

Trying to show all the dependencies in a class diagram is an exercise in futility; there are too many and they change too much. Be selective and show dependencies only when they are directly relevant to the particular topic that you want to communicate. To understand and control dependencies, you are best off using them with package diagrams (pages 89).

The most common case I use for dependencies with classes is when illustrating a transient relationship, such as when one object is passed to another as a parameter. You may see these used with keywords «parameter», «local», and «global». You may also see these keywords on associations in UML 1 models, in which case they indicate transient links, not properties. These keywords are not part of UML 2.

Dependencies can be determined by looking at code, so tools are ideal for doing dependency analysis. Getting a tool to reverse engineer pictures of dependencies is the most useful way to use this bit of the UML.

Constraint Rules

Much of what you are doing in drawing a class diagram is indicating constraints. Figure 3.1 indicates that an Order can be placed only by a single Customer. The diagram also implies that each Line Item is thought of separately: You say "40 brown widgets, 40 blue widgets, and 40 red widgets," not "120 things" on the Order. Further, the diagram says that Corporate Customers have credit limits but Personal Customers do not.

The basic constructs of association, attribute, and generalization do much to specify important constraints, but they cannot indicate every constraint. These constraints still need to be captured; the class diagram is a good place to do that.

The UML allows you to use anything to describe constraints. The only rule is that you put them inside braces ({}). You can use natural language, a programming language, or the UML's formal Object Constraint Language (OCL) [Warmer and Kleppe], which is based on predicate calculus. Using a formal notation avoids the risk of misinterpretation due to an ambiguous natural language. However, it introduces the risk of misinterpretation due to writers and readers not really understanding OCL. So unless you have readers who are comfortable with predicate calculus, I'd suggest using natural language.

Optionally, you can name a constraint by putting the name first, followed by a colon; for example, {disallow incest: husband and wife must not be siblings}.

Design by Contract

Design by Contract is a design technique developed by Bertrand Meyer [Meyer]. The technique is a central feature of the Eiffel language he developed. Design by Contract is not specific to Eiffel, however; it is a valuable technique that can be used with any programming language.

At the heart of Design by Contract is the assertion. An **assertion** is a Boolean statement that should never be false and, therefore, will be false only because of a bug. Typically, assertions are checked only during debug and are not checked during production execution. Indeed, a program should never assume that assertions are being checked.

Design by Contract uses three particular kinds of assertions: post-conditions, pre-conditions, and invariants. Pre-conditions and post-conditions apply to operations. A **post-condition** is a statement of what the world should look like after execution of an operation. For instance, if we define the operation "square root" on a number, the post-condition would take the form *input = result * result*, where *result* is the output and *input* is the input value. The post-condition is a useful way of saying what we do without saying how we do it—in other words, of separating interface from implementation.

A **pre-condition** is a statement of how we expect the world to be before we execute an operation. We might define a pre-condition for the "square root" operation of *input > = 0*. Such a pre-condition says that it is an error to invoke "square root" on a negative number and that the consequences of doing so are undefined.

On first glance, this seems a bad idea, because we should put some check somewhere to ensure that "square root" is invoked properly. The important question is who is responsible for doing so.

The pre-condition makes it explicit that the caller is responsible for checking. Without this explicit statement of responsibilities, we can get either too little checking—because both parties assume that the other is responsible—or too much—both parties check. Too much checking is a bad thing because it leads to a lot of duplicate checking code, which can significantly increase the complexity of a program. Being explicit about who is responsible helps to reduce this complexity. The danger that the caller forgets to check is reduced by the fact that assertions are usually checked during debugging and testing.

From these definitions of pre-condition and post-condition, we can see a strong definition of the term **exception**. An exception occurs when an operation is invoked with its pre-condition satisfied yet cannot return with its post-condition satisfied.

An **invariant** is an assertion about a class. For instance, an Account class may have an invariant that says that *balance == sum(entries.amount())*. The invariant is "always" true for all instances of the class. Here, "always" means "whenever the object is available to have an operation invoked on it."

In essence, this means that the invariant is added to pre-conditions and post-conditions associated with all public operations of the given class. The invariant may become false during execution of a method, but it should be restored to true by the time any other object can do anything to the receiver.

Assertions can play a unique role in subclassing. One of the dangers of inheritance is that you could redefine a subclass's operations to be inconsistent with the superclass's operations. Assertions reduce the chances of this. The invariants and post-conditions of a class must apply to all subclasses. The subclasses can choose to strengthen these assertions but cannot weaken them. The pre-condition, on the other hand, cannot be strengthened but may be weakened.

This looks odd at first, but it is important to allow dynamic binding. You should always be able to treat a subclass object as if it were an instance of the superclass, per the principle of substitutability. If a subclass strengthened its pre-condition, a superclass operation could fail when applied to the subclass.

When to Use Class Diagrams

Class diagrams are the backbone of the UML, so you will find yourself using them all the time. This chapter covers the basic concepts; Chapter 5 discusses many of the advanced concepts.

The trouble with class diagrams is that they are so rich, they can be overwhelming to use. Here are a few tips.

- Don't try to use all the notations available to you. Start with the simple stuff in this chapter: classes, associations, attributes, generalization, and constraints. Introduce other notations from Chapter 5 only when you need them.

- I've found conceptual class diagrams very useful in exploring the language of a business. For this to work, you have to work hard on keeping software out of the discussion and keeping the notation very simple.

- Don't draw models for everything; instead, concentrate on the key areas. It is better to have a few diagrams that you use and keep up to date than to have many forgotten, obsolete models.

The biggest danger with class diagrams is that you can focus exclusively on structure and ignore behavior. Therefore, when drawing class diagrams to understand software, always do them in conjunction with some form of behavioral technique. If you're going well, you'll find yourself swapping between the techniques frequently.

Where to Find Out More

All the general UML books I mentioned in Chapter 1 talk about class diagrams in more detail. Dependency management is a critical feature of larger projects. The best book on this topic is [Martin].

Chapter 4

Sequence Diagrams

Interaction diagrams describe how groups of objects collaborate in some behavior. The UML defines several forms of interaction diagram, of which the most common is the sequence diagram.

Typically, a sequence diagram captures the behavior of a single scenario. The diagram shows a number of example objects and the messages that are passed between these objects within the use case.

To begin the discussion, I'll consider a simple scenario. We have an order and are going to invoke a command on it to calculate its price. To do that, the order needs to look at all the line items on the order and determine their prices, which are based on the pricing rules of the order line's products. Having done that for all the line items, the order then needs to compute an overall discount, which is based on rules tied to the customer.

Figure 4.1 is a sequence diagram that shows one implementation of that scenario. Sequence diagrams show the interaction by showing each participant with a lifeline that runs vertically down the page and the ordering of messages by reading down the page.

One of the nice things about a sequence diagram is that I almost don't have to explain the notation. You can see that an instance of order sends getQuantity and getProduct messages to the order line. You can also see how we show the order invoking a method on itself and how that method sends getDiscountInfo to an instance of customer.

The diagram, however, doesn't show everything very well. The sequence of messages getQuantity, getProduct, getPricingDetails, and calculateBasePrice needs to be done for each order line on the order, while calculateDiscounts is invoked just once. You can't tell that from this diagram, although I'll introduce some more notation to handle that later.

Most of the time, you can think of the participants in an interaction diagram as objects, as indeed they were in UML 1. But in UML 2, their roles are much more complicated, and to explain it all fully is beyond this book. So I use the

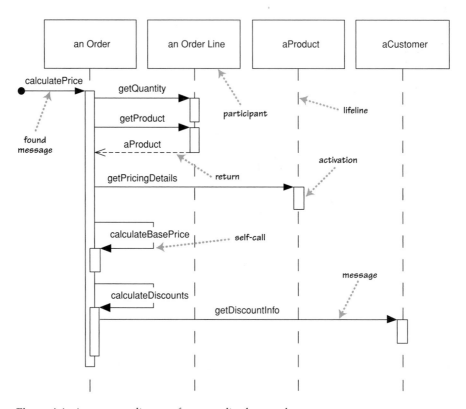

Figure 4.1 *A sequence diagram for centralized control*

term **participants,** a word that isn't used formally in the UML spec. In UML 1, participants were objects and so their names were underlined, but in UML 2, they should be shown without the underline, as I've done here.

In these diagrams, I've named the participants using the style anOrder. This works well most of the time. A fuller syntax is name : Class, where both the name and the class are optional, but you must keep the colon if you use the class. (Figure 4.4, shown on page 58, uses this style.)

Each lifeline has an activation bar that shows when the participant is active in the interaction. This corresponds to one of the participant's methods being on the stack. Activation bars are optional in UML, but I find them extremely valuable in clarifying the behavior. My one exception is when exploring a design during a design session, because they are awkward to draw on whiteboards.

Naming often is useful to correlate participants on the diagram. The call get-Product is shown returning aProduct, which is the same name, and therefore the same participant, as the aProduct that the getPricingDetails call is sent to. Note that I've used a return arrow for only this call; I did that to show the correspondence. Some people use returns for all calls, but I prefer to use them only where they add information; otherwise, they simply clutter things. Even in this case, you could probably leave the return out without confusing your reader.

The first message doesn't have a participant that sent it, as it comes from an undetermined source. It's called a **found message**.

For another approach to this scenario, take a look at Figure 4.2. The basic problem is still the same, but the way in which the participants collaborate to implement it is very different. The Order asks each Order Line to calculate its own Price. The Order Line itself further hands off the calculation to the Product; note how we show the passing of a parameter. Similarly, to calculate the discount, the Order invokes a method on the Customer. Because it needs information from the Order to do this, the Customer makes a reentrant call (getBaseValue) to the Order to get the data.

The first thing to note about these two diagrams is how clearly the sequence diagram indicates the differences in how the participants interact. This is the great strength of interaction diagrams. They aren't good at showing details of algorithms, such as loops and conditional behavior, but they make the calls between participants crystal clear and give a really good picture about which participants are doing which processing.

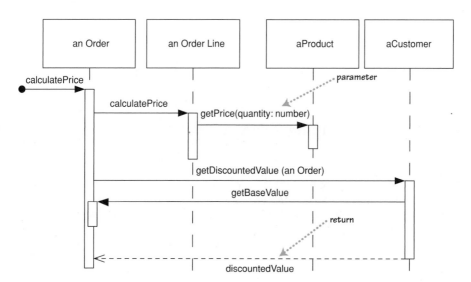

Figure 4.2 *A sequence diagram for distributed control*

The second thing to note is the clear difference in styles between the two interactions. Figure 4.1 is **centralized control,** with one participant pretty much doing all the processing and other participants there to supply data. Figure 4.2 uses **distributed control,** in which the processing is split among many participants, each one doing a little bit of the algorithm.

Both styles have their strengths and weaknesses. Most people, particularly those new to objects, are more used to centralized control. In many ways, it's simpler, as all the processing is in one place; with distributed control, in contrast, you have the sensation of chasing around the objects, trying to find the program.

Despite this, object bigots like me strongly prefer distributed control. One of the main goals of good design is to localize the effects of change. Data and behavior that accesses that data often change together. So putting the data and the behavior that uses it together in one place is the first rule of object-oriented design.

Furthermore, by distributing control, you create more opportunities for using polymorphism rather than using conditional logic. If the algorithms for product pricing are different for different types of product, the distributed control mechanism allows us to use subclasses of product to handle these variations.

In general the OO style is to use a lot of little objects with a lot of little methods that give us a lot of plug points for overriding and variation. This style is very confusing to people used to long procedures; indeed, this change is the heart of the **paradigm shift** of object orientation. It's something that's very difficult to teach. It seems that the only way to really understand it is to work in an OO environment with strongly distributed control for a while. Many people then say that they get a sudden "aha" when the style makes sense. At this point, their brains have been rewired, and they start thinking that decentralized control is actually easier.

Creating and Deleting Participants

Sequence diagrams show some extra notation for creating and deleting participants (Figure 4.3). To create a participant, you draw the message arrow directly into the participant box. A message name is optional here if you are using a constructor, but I usually mark it with "new" in any case. If the participant immediately does something once it's created, such as the query command, you start an activation right after the participant box.

Deletion of a participant is indicated by big X. A message arrow going into the X indicates one participant explicitly deleting another; an X at the end of a lifeline shows a participant deleting itself.

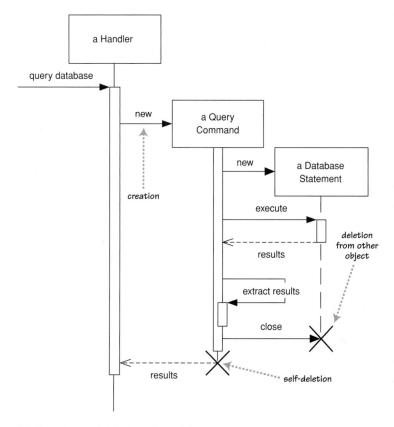

Figure 4.3 *Creation and deletion of participants*

In a garbage-collected environment, you don't delete objects directly, but it's still worth using the X to indicate when an object is no longer needed and is ready to be collected. It's also appropriate for close operations, indicating that the object isn't usable any more.

Loops, Conditionals, and the Like

A common issue with sequence diagrams is how to show looping and conditional behavior. The first thing to point out is that this isn't what sequence diagrams are good at. If you want to show control structures like this, you are better off with an activity diagram or indeed with code itself. Treat sequence diagrams as a visualization of how objects interact rather than as a way of modeling control logic.

That said, here's the notation to use. Both loops and conditionals use **interaction frames,** which are ways of marking off a piece of a sequence diagram. Figure 4.4 shows a simple algorithm based on the following pseudocode:

```
procedure dispatch
  foreach (lineitem)
    if (product.value > $10K)
      careful.dispatch
    else
      regular.dispatch
    end if
  end for
  if (needsConfirmation) messenger.confirm
end procedure
```

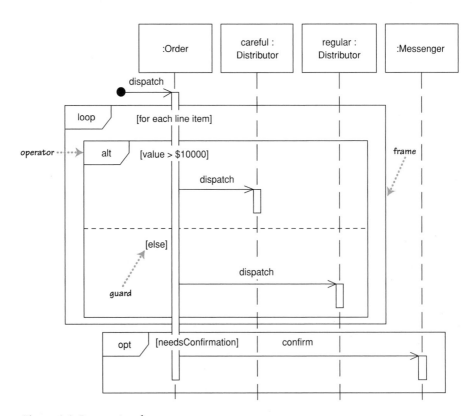

Figure 4.4 *Interaction frames*

In general, frames consist of some region of a sequence diagram that is divided into one or more fragments. Each frame has an operator and each fragment may have a guard. (Table 4.1 lists common operators for interaction frames.) To show a loop, you use the loop operator with a single fragment and put the basis of the iteration in the guard. For conditional logic, you can use an alt operator and put a condition on each fragment. Only the fragment whose guard is true will execute. If you have only one region, there is an opt operator.

Interaction frames are new in UML 2. As a result, you may see diagrams prepared before UML 2 that use a different approach; also, some people don't like the frames and prefer some of the older conventions. Figure 4.5 shows some of these unofficial tweaks.

UML 1 used iteration markers and guards. An **iteration marker** is a * added to the message name. You can add some text in square brackets to indicate the basis of the iteration. **Guards** are a conditional expression placed in square brackets and indicate that the message is sent only if the guard is true. While these notations have been dropped from sequence diagrams in UML 2, they are still legal on communication diagrams.

Although iteration markers and guards can help, they do have weaknesses. The guards can't indicate that a set of guards are mutually exclusive, such as the

Table 4.1 *Common Operators for Interaction Frames*

Operator	Meaning
alt	Alternative multiple fragments; only the one whose condition is true will execute (Figure 4.4).
opt	Optional; the fragment executes only if the supplied condition is true. Equivalent to an alt with only one trace (Figure 4.4).
par	Parallel; each fragment is run in parallel.
loop	Loop; the fragment may execute multiple times, and the guard indicates the basis of iteration (Figure 4.4).
region	Critical region; the fragment can have only one thread executing it at once.
neg	Negative; the fragment shows an invalid interaction.
ref	Reference; refers to an interaction defined on another diagram. The frame is drawn to cover the lifelines involved in the interaction. You can define parameters and a return value.
sd	Sequence diagram; used to surround an entire sequence diagram, if you wish.

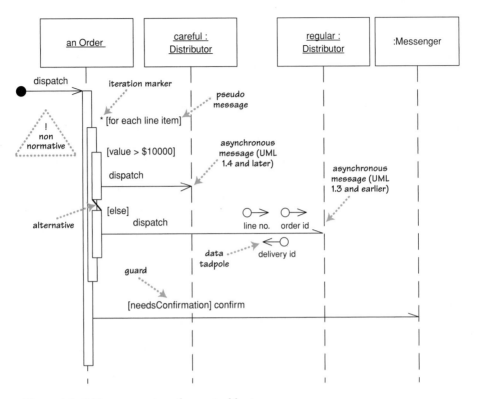

Figure 4.5 *Older conventions for control logic*

two on Figure 4.5. Both notations work only with a single message send and don't work well when several messages coming out of a single activation are within the same loop or conditional block.

To get around this last problem, an unofficial convention that's become popular is to use a **pseudomessage**, with the loop condition or the guard on a variation of the self-call notation. In Figure 4.5, I've shown this without a message arrow; some people include a message arrow, but leaving it out helps reinforce that this isn't a real call. Some also like to gray shade the pseudomessage's activation bar. If you have alternative behavior, you can show that with an alternative marker between the activations.

Although I find activations very helpful, they don't add much in the case of the dispatch method, whereby you send a message and nothing else happens within the receiver's activation. A common convention that I've shown on Figure 4.5 is to drop the activation for those simple calls.

The UML standard has no graphic device to show passing data; instead, it's shown by parameters in the message name and return arrows. **Data tadpoles** have been around in many methods to indicate the movement of data, and many people still like to use them with the UML.

All in all, although various schemes can add notation for conditional logic to sequence diagrams, I don't find that they work any better than code or at least pseudocode. In particular, I find the interaction frames very heavy, obscuring the main point of the diagram, so I prefer pseudomessages.

Synchronous and Asynchronous Calls

If you're exceptionally alert, you'll have noticed that the arrowheads in the last couple of diagrams are different from the arrowheads earlier on. That minor difference is quite important in UML 2. In UML 2, filled arrowheads show a synchronous message, while stick arrowheads show an asynchronous message.

If a caller sends a **synchronous message**, it must wait until the message is done, such as invoking a subroutine. If a caller sends an **asynchronous message,** it can continue processing and doesn't have to wait for a response. You see asynchronous calls in multithreaded applications and in message-oriented middleware. Asynchrony gives better responsiveness and reduces the temporal coupling but is harder to debug.

The arrowhead difference is very subtle; indeed, rather too subtle. It's also a backward-incompatible change introduced in UML 1.4, before then an asynchronous message was shown with the half-stick arrowhead, as in Figure 4.5.

I think that this arrowhead distinction is too subtle. If you want to highlight asynchronous messages, I would recommend using the obsolete half-stick arrowhead, which draws the eye much better to an important distinction. If you're reading a sequence diagram, beware of making assumptions about synchrony from the arrowheads unless you're sure that the author is intentionally making the distinction.

When to Use Sequence Diagrams

You should use sequence diagrams when you want to look at the behavior of several objects within a single use case. Sequence diagrams are good at showing collaborations among the objects; they are not so good at precise definition of the behavior.

If you want to look at the behavior of a single object across many use cases, use a state diagram (see Chapter 10). If you want to look at behavior across many use cases or many threads, consider an activity diagram (see Chapter 11).

If you want to explore multiple alternative interactions quickly, you may be better off with CRC cards, as that avoids a lot of drawing and erasing. It's often handy to have a CRC card session to explore design alternatives and then use sequence diagrams to capture any interactions that you want to refer to later.

Other useful forms of interaction diagrams are communication diagrams, for showing connections; and timing diagrams, for showing timing constraints.

CRC Cards

One of the most valuable techniques in coming up with a good OO design is to explore object interactions, because it focuses on behavior rather than data. CRC (Class-Responsibility-Collaboration) diagrams, invented by Ward Cunningham in the late 1980s, have stood the test of time as a highly effective way to do this (Figure 4.6). Although they aren't part of the UML, they are a very popular technique among skilled object designers.

To use CRC cards, you and your colleagues gather around a table. Take various scenarios and act them out with the cards, picking them up in the air when they are active and moving them to suggest how they send messages to each other and pass them around. This technique is almost impossible to describe in a book yet is easily demonstrated; the best way to learn it is to have someone who has done it show it to you.

responsibility	class name		collaboration
Order			
Check if items in stock		Order Line	
Determine price		Customer	
Check for valid payment			
Dispatch to delivery address			

Figure 4.6 *A sample CRC card*

An important part of CRC thinking is identifying responsibilities. A **responsibility** is a short sentence that summarizes something that an object should do: an action the object performs, some knowledge the object maintains, or some important decisions the object makes. The idea is that you should be able to take any class and summarize it with a handful of responsibilities. Doing that can help you think more clearly about the design of your classes.

The second C refers to **collaborators**: the other classes that this class needs to work with. This gives you some idea of the links between classes—still at a high level.

One of the chief benefits of CRC cards is that they encourage animated discussion among the developers. When you are working through a use case to see how classes will implement it, the interaction diagrams in this chapter can be slow to draw. Usually, you need to consider alternatives; with diagrams, the alternatives can take too long to draw and rub out. With CRC cards, you model the interaction by picking up the cards and moving them around. This allows you to quickly consider alternatives.

As you do this, you form ideas about responsibilities and write them on the cards. Thinking about responsibilities is important, because it gets you away from the notion of classes as dumb data holders and eases the team members toward understanding the higher-level behavior of each class. A responsibility may correspond to an operation, to an attribute, or, more likely, to an undetermined clump of attributes and operations.

A common mistake I see people make is generating long lists of low-level responsibilities. But doing so misses the point. The responsibilities should easily fit on one card. Ask yourself whether the class should be split or whether the responsibilities would be better stated by rolling them up into higher-level statements.

Many people stress the importance of role playing, whereby each person on the team plays the role of one or more classes. I've never seen Ward Cunningham do that, and I find that role playing gets in the way.

Books have been written on CRC, but I've found that they never really get to the heart of the technique. The original paper on CRC, written with Kent Beck, is [Beck and Cunningham]. To learn more about both CRC cards and responsibilities in design, take a look at [Wirfs-Brock].

Chapter 5

Class Diagrams: Advanced Concepts

The concepts described in Chapter 3 correspond to the key notations in class diagrams. Those concepts are the first ones to understand and become familiar with, as they will comprise 90 percent of your effort in building class diagrams.

The class diagram technique, however, has bred dozens of notations for additional concepts. I find that I don't use these all the time, but they are handy when they are appropriate. I'll discuss them one at a time and point out some of the issues in using them.

You'll probably find this chapter somewhat heavy going. The good news is that during your first pass through the book, you can safely skip this chapter and come back to it later.

Keywords

One of the challenges of a graphical language is that you have to remember what the symbols mean. With too many, users find it very difficult to remember what all the symbols mean. So the UML often tries to reduce the number of symbols and use keywords instead. If you find that you need a modeling construct that isn't in the UML but is similar to something that is, use the symbol of the existing UML construct but mark it with a keyword to show that you have something different

An example of this is the interface. A UML **interface** (page 69) is a class that has only public operations, with no method bodies. This corresponds to interfaces in Java, COM (Component Object Module), and CORBA. Because it's a special kind of class, it is shown using the class icon with the keyword «interface». Keywords are usually shown as text between guillemets. As an alternative to keywords, you can use special icons, but then you run into the issue of everyone having to remember what they mean.

Some keywords, such as {abstract}, show up in curly brackets. It's never really clear what should technically be in guillemets and what should be in curlies. Fortunately, if you get it wrong, only serious UML weenies will notice—or care.

Some keywords are so common that they often get abbreviated: «interface» often gets abbreviated to «I» and {abstract} to {A}. Such abbreviations are very useful, particularly on whiteboards, but nonstandard, so if you use them, make sure you find a spot to spell out what they mean.

In UML 1, the guillemets were used mainly for **stereotypes**. In UML 2, stereotypes are defined very tightly, and describing what is and isn't a stereotype is beyond the scope of this book. However, because of UML 1, many people use the term *stereotype* to mean the same as *keyword*, although that is no longer correct.

Stereotypes are used as part of profiles. A **profile** takes a part of the UML and extends it with a coherent group of stereotypes for a particular purpose, such as business modeling. The full semantics of profiles are beyond this book. Unless you are into serious meta-model design, you're unlikely to need to create one yourself. You're more likely to use one created for a specific modeling purpose, but fortunately, use of a profile doesn't require you to know the gory details of how they are tied into the meta-model.

Responsibilities

Often, it's handy to show responsibilities (page 63) on a class in a class diagram. The best way to show them is as comment strings in their own compartment in the class (Figure 5.1). You can name the compartment, if you wish, but I usually don't, as there's rarely any potential for confusion.

Static Operations and Attributes

The UML refers to an operation or an attribute that applies to a class rather than to an instance as **static**. This is equivalent to static members in C-based languages. Static features are <u>underlined</u> on a class diagram (see Figure 5.2).

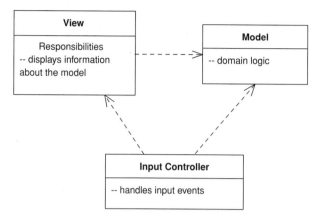

Figure 5.1 *Showing responsibilities in a class diagram*

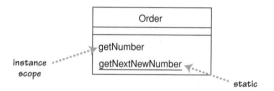

Figure 5.2 *Static notation*

Aggregation and Composition

One of the most frequent sources of confusion in the UML is aggregation and composition. It's easy to explain glibly: **Aggregation** is the part-of relationship. It's like saying that a car has an engine and wheels as its parts. This sounds good, but the difficult thing is considering what the difference is between aggregation and association.

In the pre-UML days, people were usually rather vague on what was aggregation and what was association. Whether vague or not, they were always inconsistent with everyone else. As a result, many modelers think that aggregation is important, although for different reasons. So the UML included aggregation (Figure 5.3) but with hardly any semantics. As Jim Rumbaugh says, "Think of it as a modeling placebo" [Rumbaugh, UML Reference].

Figure 5.3 *Aggregation*

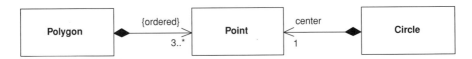

Figure 5.4 *Composition*

As well as aggregation, the UML has the more defined property of **composition**. In Figure 5.4, an instance of Point may be part of a polygon or may be the center of a circle, but it cannot be both. The general rule is that, although a class may be a component of many other classes, any instance must be a component of only one owner. The class diagram may show multiple classes of potential owners, but any instance has only a single object as its owner.

You'll note that I don't show the reverse multiplicities in Figure 5.4. In most cases, as here, it's 0..1. Its only other possible value is 1, for cases in which the component class is designed so that it can have only one other class as its owner.

The "no sharing" rule is the key to composition. Another assumption is that if you delete the polygon, it should automatically ensure that any owned Points also are deleted.

Composition is a good way of showing properties that own by value, properties to value objects (page 73), or properties that have a strong and somewhat exclusive ownership of particular other components. Aggregation is strictly meaningless; as a result, I recommend that you ignore it in your own diagrams. If you see it in other people's diagrams, you'll need to dig deeper to find out what they mean by it. Different authors and teams use it for very different purposes.

Derived Properties

Derived properties can be calculated based on other values. When we think about a date range (Figure 5.5), we can think of three properties: the start date,

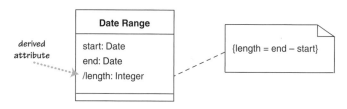

Figure 5.5 *Derived attribute in a time period*

the end date, and the number of days in the period. These values are linked, so we can think of the length as being derived from the other two values.

Derivation in software perspectives can be interpreted in a couple of different ways. You can use derivation to indicate the difference between a calculated value and a stored value. In this case, we would interpret Figure 5.5 as indicating that the start and end are stored but that the length is computed. Although this is a common use, I'm not so keen, because it reveals too much of the internals of DateRange.

My preferred thinking is that it indicates a constraint between values. In this case, we are saying that the constraint among the three values holds, but it isn't important which of the three values is computed. In this case, the choice of which attribute to mark as derived is arbitrary and strictly unnecessary, but it's useful to help remind people of the constraint. This usage also makes sense with conceptual diagrams.

Derivation can also be applied to properties using association notation. In this case, you simply mark the name with a /.

Interfaces and Abstract Classes

An **abstract class** is a class that cannot be directly instantiated. Instead, you instantiate an instance of a subclass. Typically, an abstract class has one or more operations that are abstract. An **abstract operation** has no implementation; it is pure declaration so that clients can bind to the abstract class.

The most common way to indicate an abstract class or operation in the UML is to *italicize* the name. You can also make properties abstract, indicating an abstract property or accessor methods. Italics are tricky to do on a whiteboards, so you can use the label: {abstract}.

An interface is a class that has no implementation; that is, all its features are abstract. Interfaces correspond directly to interfaces in C# and Java and are a common idiom in other typed languages. You mark an interface with the key-word «interface».

Classes have two kinds of relationships with interfaces: providing and requiring. A class **provides an interface** if it is substitutable for the interface. In Java and .NET, a class can do that by implementing the interface or implementing a subtype of the interface. In C++, you subclass the class that is the interface.

A class **requires an interface** if it needs an instance of that interface in order to work. Essentially, this is having a dependency on the interface.

Figure 5.6 shows these relationships in action, based on a few collection classes from Java. I might write an Order class that has a list of line items. Because I'm using a list, the Order class is dependent on the List interface. Let's assume that it uses the methods equals, add, and get. When the objects connect,

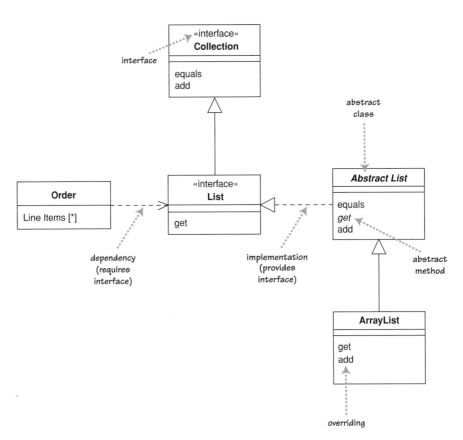

Figure 5.6 *A Java example of interfaces and an abstract class*

the Order will actually use an instance of ArrayList but need not know that in order to use those three methods, as they are all part of the List interface.

The ArrayList itself is a subclass of the AbstractList class. AbstractList provides some, but not all, the implementation of the List behavior. In particular, the get method is abstract. As a result, ArrayList implements get but also overrides some of the other operations on AbstractList. In this case, it overrides add but is happy to inherit the implementation of equals.

Why don't I simply avoid this and have Order use ArrayList directly? By using the interface, I allow myself the advantage of making it easier to change implementations later on if I need to. Another implementation may provide performance improvements, some database interaction features, or other benefits. By programming to the interface rather than to the implementation, I avoid having to change all the code should I need a different implementation of List. You should always try to program to an interface like this; always use the most general type you can.

I should also point out a pragmatic wrinkle in this. When programmers use a collection like this, they usually initialize the collection with a declaration, like this:

```
private List lineItems = new ArrayList();
```

Note that this strictly introduces a dependency from Order to the concrete ArrayList. In theory, this is a problem, but people don't worry about it in practice. Because the type of lineItems is declared as List, no other part of the Order class is dependent on ArrayList. Should we change the implementation, there's only this one line of initialization code that we need to worry about. It's quite common to refer to a concrete class once during creation but to use only the interface afterward.

The full notation of Figure 5.6 is one way to notate interfaces. Figure 5.7 shows a more compact notation. The fact that ArrayList implements List and Collection is shown by having ball icons (often referred to as lollipops) out of it. The fact that Order requires a List interface is shown by the socket icon. The connection is made by a dependency arrow.

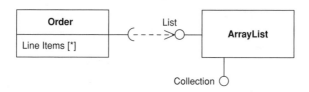

Figure 5.7 *Ball-and-socket notation*

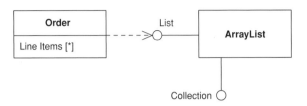

Figure 5.8 *Older dependencies with lollipops*

UML has used the lollipop notation for a while, but the socket notation is new to UML 2. The socket is also optional, so you'll often see diagrams use the style of Figure 5.8. (When you are using parts within Composite Structures, discussed in Chapter 13, you can mate the ball and socket—but you can only do this with parts.)

Any class is a mix of an interface and an implementation. Therefore, we may often see an object used through the interface of one of its superclasses. Strictly, it wouldn't be legal to use the lollipop notation for a superclass, as the superclass is a class, not a pure interface. But I bend these rules for clarity.

As well as on class diagrams, people have found lollipops useful elsewhere. One of the perennial problems with interaction diagrams is that they don't provide a very good visualization for polymorphic behavior. Although it's not normative usage, you can indicate this along the lines of Figure 5.9. Here, we can see that, although we have an instance of Salesman, which is used as such by the Bonus Calculator, the Pay Period object uses the Salesman only through its Employee interface. (You can do the same trick with communication diagrams.)

Read-Only and Frozen

On page 37, I described the {readOnly} keyword. You use this keyword to mark a property that can only be read by clients and that cannot be updated. Similar yet different is the {frozen} keyword from UML 1. A property is **frozen** if it cannot change during the lifetime of an object; such properties are often called immutable. Although it was dropped from UML 2, {frozen} is a very useful concept, so I would continue to use it. As well as marking individual properties as frozen, you can apply the keyword to a class to indicate that all properties of all instances are frozen. (I have heard that frozen may well be reinstated shortly.)

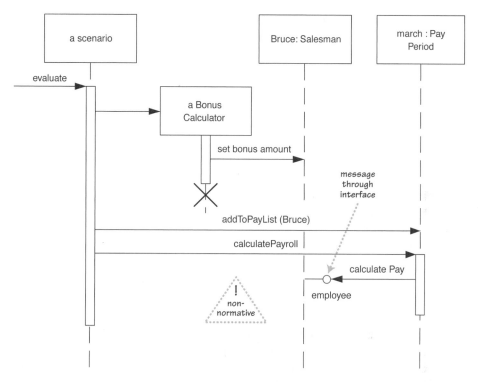

Figure 5.9 *Using a lollipop to show polymorphism in a sequence diagram*

Reference Objects and Value Objects

One of the common things said about objects is that they have identity. This is true, but it is not quite as simple as that. In practice, you find that identity is important for reference objects but not so important for value objects.

Reference objects are such things as Customer. Here, identity is very important because you usually want only one software object to designate a customer in the real world. Any object that references a Customer object will do so through a reference, or pointer; all objects that reference this Customer will reference the same software object. That way, changes to a Customer are available to all users of the Customer.

If you have two references to a Customer and wish to see whether they are the same, you usually compare their identities. Copies may be disallowed; if they are allowed, they tend to be made rarely, perhaps for archive purposes or for replication across a network. If copies are made, you need to sort out how to synchronize changes.

Value objects are such things as Date. You often have multiple value objects representing the same object in the real world. For example, it is normal to have hundreds of objects that designate 1-Jan-04. These are all interchangeable copies. New dates are created and destroyed frequently.

If you have two dates and wish to see whether they are the same, you don't look at their identities but rather at the values they represent. This usually means that you have to write an equality test operator, which for dates would make a test on year, month, and day—or whatever the internal representation is. Each object that references 1-Jan-04 usually has its own dedicated object, but you can also share dates.

Value objects should be immutable; in other words, you should not be able to take a date object of 1-Jan-04 and change the same date object to be 2-Jan-04. Instead, you should create a new 2-Jan-04 object and use that instead. The reason is that if the date were shared, you would update another object's date in an unpredictable way, a problem referred to as **aliasing**.

In days gone by, the difference between reference objects and value objects was clearer. Value objects were the built-in values of the type system. Now you can extend the type system with your own classes, so this issue requires more thought.

The UML uses the concept of **data type**, which is shown as a keyword on the class symbol. Strictly, data type isn't the same as value object, as data types can't have identity. Value objects may have an identity, but don't use it for equality. Primitives in Java would be data types, but dates would not, although they would be value objects.

If it's important to highlight them, I use composition when associating with a value object. You can also use a keyword on a value type; common conventional ones I see are «value» or «struct».

Qualified Associations

A **qualified association** is the UML equivalent of a programming concept variously known as associative arrays, maps, hashes, and dictionaries. Figure 5.10 shows a way that uses a qualifier to represent the association between the Order and Order Line classes. The qualifier says that in connection with an Order, there may be one Order Line for each instance of Product.

Figure 5.10 *Qualified association*

From a software perspective, this qualified association would imply an interface along the lines of

```
class Order ...
  public OrderLine getLineItem(Product aProduct);
  public void addLineItem(Number amount, Product forProduct);
```

Thus, all access to a given Order Line requires a Product as an argument, suggesting an implementation using a key and value data structure.

It's common for people to get confused about the multiplicities of a qualified association. In Figure 5.10, an Order may have many Line Items, but the multiplicity of the qualified association is the multiplicity in the context of the qualifier. So the diagram says that an Order has 0..1 Line Items per Product. A multiplicity of 1 would indicate that Order would have to have a Line Item for every instance of Product. A * would indicate that you would have multiple Line Items per Product but that access to the Line Items is indexed by Product.

In conceptual modeling, I use the qualifier construct only to show constraints along the lines of "single Order Line per Product on Order."

Classification and Generalization

I often hear people talk about subtyping as the *is a* relationship. I urge you to beware of that way of thinking. The problem is that the phrase *is a* can mean different things.

Consider the following phrases.

1. Shep is a Border Collie.
2. A Border Collie is a Dog.
3. Dogs are Animals.
4. A Border Collie is a Breed.
5. Dog is a Species.

Now try combining the phrases. If I combine phrases 1 and 2, I get "Shep is a Dog"; 2 and 3 taken together yield "Border Collies are Animals." And 1 plus 2 plus 3 gives me "Shep is an Animal." So far, so good. Now try 1 and 4: "Shep is a Breed." The combination of 2 and 5 is "A Border Collie is a Species." These are not so good.

Why can I combine some of these phrases and not others? The reason is that some are **classification**—the object Shep is an instance of the type Border Collie—and some are **generalization**—the type Border Collie is a subtype of the type Dog. Generalization is transitive; classification is not. I can combine a classification followed by a generalization but not vice versa.

I make this point to get you to be wary of *is a*. Using it can lead to inappropriate use of subclassing and confused responsibilities. Better tests for subtyping in this case would be the phrases "Dogs are kinds of Animals" and "Every instance of a Border Collie is an instance of a Dog."

The UML uses the generalization symbol to show generalization. If you need to show classification, use a dependency with the «instantiate» keyword.

Multiple and Dynamic Classification

Classification refers to the relationship between an object and its type. Mainstream programming languages assume that an object belongs to a single class. But there are more options to classification than that.

In **single classification**, an object belongs to a single type, which may inherit from supertypes. In **multiple classification**, an object may be described by several types that are not necessarily connected by inheritance.

Multiple classification is different from multiple inheritance. Multiple inheritance says that a type may have many supertypes but that a single type must be defined for each object. Multiple classification allows multiple types for an object without defining a specific type for the purpose.

For example, consider a person subtyped as either man or woman, doctor or nurse, patient or not (see Figure 5.11). Multiple classification allows an object to have any of these types assigned to it in any allowable combination, without the need for types to be defined for all the legal combinations.

If you use multiple classification, you need to be sure that you make it clear which combinations are legal. UML 2 does this by placing each generalization relationship into a **generalization set**. On the class diagram, you label the generalization arrowhead with the name of the generalization set, which in UML 1

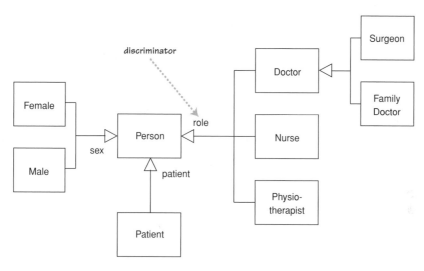

Figure 5.11 *Multiple classification*

was called the discriminator. Single classification corresponds to a single generalization set with no name.

Generalization sets are by default disjoint: Any instance of the supertype may be an instance of only one of the subtypes within that set. If you roll up generalizations into a single arrow, they must all be part of the same generalization set, as shown in Figure 5.11. Alternatively, you can have several arrows with the same text label.

To illustrate, note the following legal combinations of subtypes in the diagram: (Female, Patient, Nurse); (Male, Physiotherapist); (Female, Patient); and (Female, Doctor, Surgeon). The combination (Patient, Doctor, Nurse) is illegal because it contains two types from the role generalization set.

Another question is whether an object may change its class. For example, when a bank account is overdrawn, it substantially changes its behavior. Specifically, several operations, including "withdraw" and "close," get overridden.

Dynamic classification allows objects to change class within the subtyping structure; **static classification** does not. With static classification, a separation is made between types and states; dynamic classification combines these notions.

Should you use multiple, dynamic classification? I believe that it is useful for conceptual modeling. For software perspectives, however, the distance between it and the implementations is too much of a leap. In the vast majority of UML diagrams, you'll see only single static classification, so that should be your default.

Association Class

Association classes allow you to add attributes, operations, and other features to associations, as shown in Figure 5.12. We can see from the diagram that a person may attend many meetings. We need to keep information about how awake that person was; we can do this by adding the attribute attentiveness to the association.

Figure 5.13 shows another way to represent this information: Make Attendance a full class in its own right. Note how the multiplicities have moved.

What benefit do you gain with the association class to offset the extra notation you have to remember? The association class adds an extra constraint, in that there can be only one instance of the association class between any two participating objects. I feel the need for another example.

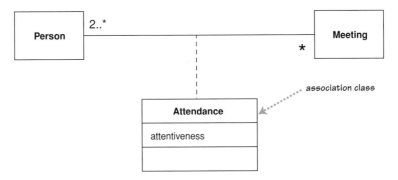

Figure 5.12 *Association class*

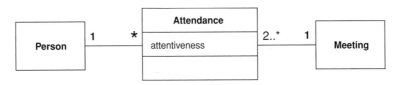

Figure 5.13 *Promoting an association class to a full class*

Take a look at the two diagrams in Figure 5.14. These diagrams have much the same form. However, we can imagine one Company playing different roles in the same Contract, but it's harder to imagine a Person having multiple competencies in the same skill; indeed, you would probably consider that an error.

In the UML, only the latter case is legal. You can have only one competency for each combination of Person and Skill. The top diagram in Figure 5.14 would not allow a Company to have more than one Role on a single contract. If you need to allow this, you need to make Role a full class, in the style of Figure 5.13.

Implementing association classes isn't terribly obvious. My advice is to implement an association class as if it were a full class but to provide methods that get information to the classes linked by the association class. So for Figure 5.12, I would see the following methods on Person:

```
class Person
  List getAttendances()
  List getMeetings()
```

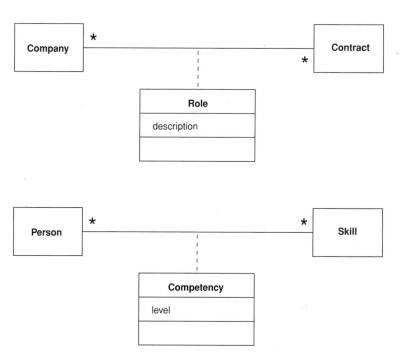

Figure 5.14 *Association class subtleties (Role should probably not be an association class)*

This way, a client of Person can get hold of the people at the meeting; if they want details, they can get the Attendances themselves. If you do this, remember to enforce the constraint that there can be only one Attendance object for any pair of Person and Meeting. You should place a check in whichever method creates the Attendance.

You often find this kind of construct with historical information, such as in Figure 5.15. However, I find that creating extra classes or association classes can make the model tricky to understand, as well as tilt the implementation in a particular direction that's often unsuitable.

If I have this kind of temporal information, I use a «temporal» keyword on the association (see Figure 5.16). The model indicates that a Person may work for only a single Company at one time. Over time, however, a Person may work for several Companies. This suggests an interface along the lines of:

```
class Person ...
  Company getEmployer();//get current employer
  Company getEmployer(Date);//get employer at a given date
  void changeEmployer(Company newEmployer,Date changeDate);
  void leaveEmployer (Date changeDate);
```

The «temporal» keyword is not part of the UML, but I mention it here for two reasons. First, it is a notion I have found useful on several occasions in my modeling career. Second, it shows how you can use keywords to extend the UML. You can read a lot more about this at **http://martinfowler.com/ap2/ timeNarrative.html**.

Figure 5.15 *Using a class for a temporal relationship*

Figure 5.16 «Temporal» *keyword for associations*

Template (Parameterized) Class

Several languages, most noticeably C++, have the notion of a **parameterized class**, or **template**. (Templates are on the list to be included in Java and C# in the near future.)

This concept is most obviously useful for working with collections in a strongly typed language. This way, you can define behavior for sets in general by defining a template class Set.

```
class Set <T> {
  void insert (T newElement);
  void remove (T anElement);
```

When you have done this, you can use the general definition to make Set classes for more specific elements:

```
Set <Employee> employeeSet;
```

You declare a template class in the UML by using the notation shown in Figure 5.17. The T in the diagram is a placeholder for the type parameter. (You may have more than one.)

A use of a parameterized class, such as Set<Employee>, is called a **derivation**. You can show a derivation in two ways. The first way mirrors the C++ syntax (see Figure 5.18). You describe the derivation expression within angle brackets in the form <parameter-name::parameter-value>. If there's only one parameter, conventional use often omits the parameter name. The alternative notation (see Figure 5.19) reinforces the link to the template and allows you to rename the bound element.

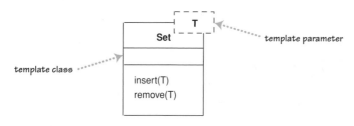

Figure 5.17 *Template class*

```
┌─────────────────────┐
│                     │
│   Set <T::Employee> │
│                     │
└─────────────────────┘
```

Figure 5.18 *Bound element (version 1)*

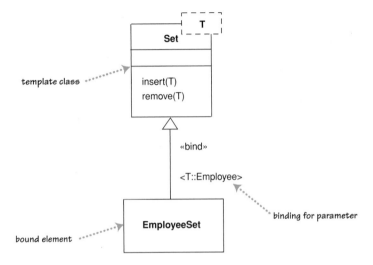

Figure 5.19 *Bound element (version 2)*

The «bind» keyword is a stereotype on the refinement relationship. This relationship indicates that EmployeeSet will conform to the interface of Set. You can think of the EmployeeSet as a subtype of Set. This fits the other way of implementing type-specific collections, which is to declare all appropriate subtypes.

Using a derivation is *not* the same as subtyping, however. You are not allowed to add features to the bound element, which is completely specified by its template; you are adding only restricting type information. If you want to add features, you must create a subtype.

Enumerations

Enumerations (Figure 5.20) are used to show a fixed set of values that don't have any properties other than their symbolic value. They are shown as the class with the «enumeration» keyword.

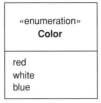

Figure 5.20 *Enumeration*

Active Class

An **active class** has instances, each of which executes and controls its own thread of control. Method invocations may execute in a client's thread or in the active object's thread. A good example of this is a command processor that accepts command objects from the outside and then executes the commands within its own thread of control.

The notation for active classes has changed from UML 1 to UML 2, as shown in Figure 5.21. In UML 2, an active class has extra vertical lines on the side; in UML 1, it had a thick border and was called an active object.

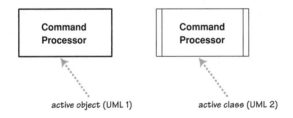

Figure 5.21 *Active class*

Visibility

Visibility is a subject that is simple in principle but has complex subtleties. The simple idea is that any class has public and private elements. Public elements can be used by any other class; private elements can be used only by the owning class. However, each language makes its own rules. Although many languages use such terms as *public*, *private*, and *protected*, they mean different things in different languages. These differences are small, but they lead to confusion, especially for those of us who use more than one language.

The UML tries to address this without getting into a horrible tangle. Essentially, within the UML, you can tag any attribute or operation with a visibility indicator. You can use any marker you like, and its meaning is language dependent. However, the UML provides four abbreviations for visibility: + (public), – (private), ~ (package), and # (protected). These four levels are used within the UML meta-model and are defined within it, but their definitions vary subtly from those in other languages.

When you are using visibility, use the rules of the language in which you are working. When you are looking at a UML model from elsewhere, be wary of the meanings of the visibility markers, and be aware of how those meanings can change from language to language.

Most of the time, I don't draw visibility markers in diagrams; I use them only if I need to highlight the differences in visibility of certain features. Even then, I can mostly get away with + and –, which at least are easy to remember.

Messages

Standard UML does not show any information about message calls on class diagrams. However, I've sometimes seen conventional diagrams like Figure 5.22.

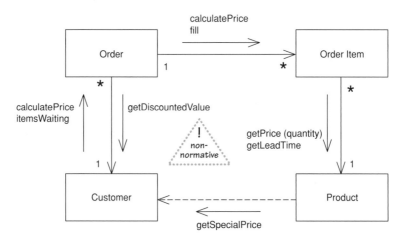

Figure 5.22 *Classes with messages*

These add arrows to the sides of associations. The arrows are labeled with the messages that one object sends to another. Because you don't need an association to a class to send a message to it, you may also need to add a dependency arrow to show messages between classes that aren't associated.

This message information spans multiple use cases, so they aren't numbered to show sequences, unlike communication diagrams.

Chapter 6

Object Diagrams

An **object diagram** is a snapshot of the objects in a system at a point in time. Because it shows instances rather than classes, an object diagram is often called an instance diagram.

You can use an object diagram to show an example configuration of objects. (See Figure 6.1, which shows a set of classes, and Figure 6.2, which shows an associated set of objects.) This latter use is very useful when the possible connections between objects are complicated.

You can tell that the elements in Figure 6.2 are instances because the names are underlined. Each name takes the form `instance name : class name`. Both parts of the name are optional, so `John`, `:Person`, and `aPerson` are legal names. If you use only the class name, you must include the colon. You can show values for attributes and links, as in Figure 6.2.

Strictly, the elements of an object diagram are instance specifications rather than true instances. The reason is that it's legal to leave mandatory attributes empty or to show instance specifications of abstract classes. You can think of an **instance specification** as a partly defined instance.

Another way of looking at an object diagram is as a communication diagram (page 131) without messages.

When to Use Object Diagrams

Object diagrams are useful for showing examples of objects connected together. In many situations, you can define a structure precisely with a class diagram, but the structure is still difficult to understand. In these situations, a couple of object diagram examples can make all the difference.

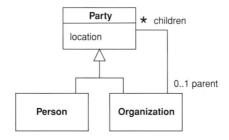

Figure 6.1 *Class diagram of Party composition structure*

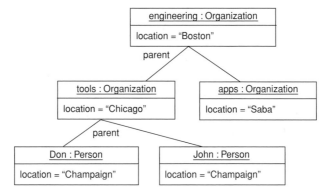

Figure 6.2 *Object diagram showing example instances of Party*

Chapter 7

Package Diagrams

Classes represent the basic form of structuring an object-oriented system. Although they are wonderfully useful, you need something more to structure large systems, which may have hundreds of classes.

A **package** is a grouping construct that allows you to take any construct in the UML and group its elements together into higher-level units. Its most common use is to group classes, and that's the way I'm describing it here, but remember that you can use packages for every other bit of the UML as well.

In a UML model, each class is a member of a single package. Packages can also be members of other packages, so you are left with a hierarchic structure in which top-level packages get broken down into subpackages with their own subpackages and so on until the hierarchy bottoms out in classes. A package can contain both subpackages and classes.

In programming terms, packages correspond to such grouping constructs as packages (in Java) and namespaces (in C++ and .NET).

Each package represents a **namespace**, which means that every class must have a unique name within its owning package. If I want to create a class called Date, and a Date class is already in the System package, I can have my Date class as long as I put it in a separate package. To make it clear which is which, I can use a **fully qualified name,** that is, a name that shows the owning package structure. You use double colons to show package names in UML, so the dates might be System::Date and MartinFowler::Util::Date.

In diagrams, packages are shown with a tabbed folder, as in Figure 7.1. You can simply show the package name or show the contents too. At any point, you can use fully qualified names or simply regular names. Showing the contents with class icons allows you to show all the details of a class, even to the point of showing a class diagram within the package. Simply listing the names makes sense when all you want to do is indicate which classes are in which packages.

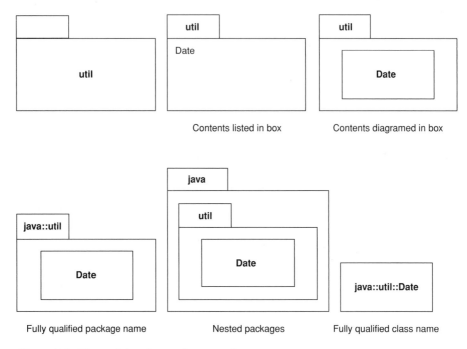

Figure 7.1 *Ways of showing packages on diagrams*

It's quite common to see a class labeled something like Date (from java.util) rather than the fully qualified form. This style is a convention that was done a lot by Rational Rose; it isn't part of the standard.

The UML allows classes in a package to be public or private. A public class is part of the interface of the package and can be used by classes in other packages; a private class is hidden. Different programming environments have different rules about visibility between their packaging constructs; you should follow the convention of your programming environment, even if it means bending the UML's rules.

A useful technique here is to reduce the interface of the package by exporting only a small subset of the operations associated with the package's public classes. You can do this by giving all classes private visibility, so that they can be seen only by other classes in the same package, and by adding extra public classes for the public behavior. These extra classes, called *Facades* [Gang of Four], then delegate public operations to their shyer companions in the package.

How do you choose which classes to put in which packages? This is actually quite an involved question that needs a good bit of design skill to answer. Two useful principles are the Common Closure Principle and Common Reuse Principle [Martin]. The Common Closure Principle says that the classes in a package should need changing for similar reasons. The Common Reuse Principle says that classes in a package should all be reused together. Many of the reasons for grouping classes in packages have to do with the dependencies between the packages, which I'll come to next.

Packages and Dependencies

A **package diagram** shows packages and their dependencies. I introduced the concept of dependency on page 47. If you have packages for presentation and domain, you have a dependency from the presentation package to the domain package if any class in the presentation package has a dependency to any class in the domain package. In this way, interpackage dependencies summarize the dependencies between their contents.

The UML has many varieties of dependency, each with particular semantics and stereotype. I find it easier to begin with the unstereotyped dependency and use the more particular dependencies only if I need to, which I hardly ever do.

In a medium to large system, plotting a package diagram can be one of the most valuable things you can do to control the large-scale structure of the system. Ideally, this diagram should be generated from the code base itself, so that you can see what is really there in the system.

A good package structure has a clear flow to the dependencies, a concept that's difficult to define but often easier to recognize. Figure 7.2 shows a sample package diagram for an enterprise application, one that is well-structured and has a clear flow.

Often, you can identify a clear flow because all the dependencies run in a single direction. Although that is a good indicator of a well-structured system, the data mapper packages of Figure 7.2 show an exception to that rule of thumb. The data mapper packages act as an insulating layer between the domain and database packages, an example of the Mapper pattern [Fowler, P of EAA].

Many authors say that there should be no cycles in the dependencies (the Acyclic Dependency Principle [Martin]). I don't treat that as an absolute rule, but I do think that cycles should be localized and that, in particular, you shouldn't have cycles that cross layers.

The more dependencies coming into a package, the more stable the package's interface needs to be, as any change in its interface will ripple into all the packages that are dependent on it (the Stable Dependencies Principle [Martin]). So in Figure 7.2, the asset domain package needs a more stable interface than the

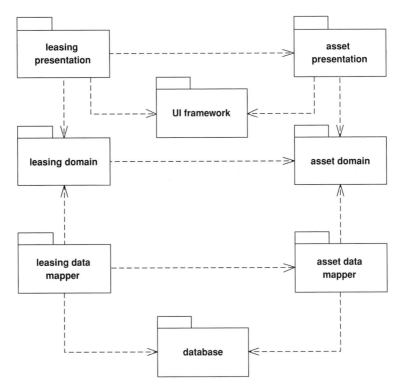

Figure 7.2 *Package diagram for an enterprise application*

leasing data mapper package. Often, you'll find that the more stable packages tend to have a higher proportion of interfaces and abstract classes (the Stable Abstractions Principle [Martin].

The dependency relationships are not transitive (page 48). To see why this is important for dependencies, look at Figure 7.2 again. If a class in the asset domain package changes, we may have a change to classes within the leasing domain package. But this change does not necessarily ripple through to the leasing presentation. (It ripples only if the leasing domain changes its interface.)

Some packages are used in so many places that it would be a mess to draw all the dependency lines to them. In this case, a convention is to use a keyword, such as «global», on the package.

UML packages also define constructs to allow packages to import and merge classes from one package into another, using dependencies with keywords to notate this. However, rules for this kind of thing vary greatly with programming languages. On the whole, I find the general notion of dependencies to be far more useful in practice.

Package Aspects

If you think about Figure 7.2, you'll realize that the diagram has two kinds of structures. One is a structure of layers in the application: presentation, domain, data mapper, and database. The other is a structure of subject areas: leasing and assets.

You can make this more apparent by separating the two aspects, as in Figure 7.3. With this diagram, you can clearly see each aspect. However, these two aspects aren't true packages, because you can't assign classes to a single package. (You would have to pick one from each aspect.) This problem mirrors

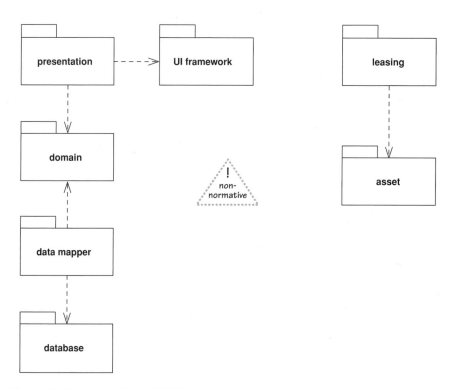

Figure 7.3 *Separating Figure 7.2 into two aspects*

the problem in the hierarchic namespaces in programming languages. Although diagrams like Figure 7.3 are nonstandard UML, they are often very helpful in explaining the structure of a complex application.

Implementing Packages

Often, you'll see a case in which one package defines an interface that can be implemented by a number of other packages, such as that of Figure 7.4. In this case, the realization relationship indicates that the database gateway defines an interface and that the other gateway classes provide an implementation. In practice, this would mean that the database gateway package contains interfaces and abstract classes that are fully implemented by the other packages.

It's quite common for an interface and its implementation to be in separate packages. Indeed, a client package often contains an interface for another package to implement: the same notion of required interface that I discussed on page 70.

Imagine that we want to provide some user interface (UI) controls to turn things on and off. We want this to work with a lot of different things, such as heaters and lights. The UI controls need to invoke methods on the heater, but we don't want the controls to have a dependency to the heater. We can avoid this dependency by defining in the controls package an interface that is then implemented by any class that wants to work with these controls, as in Figure 7.5. This is an example of the pattern Separated Interface [Fowler, P of EAA].

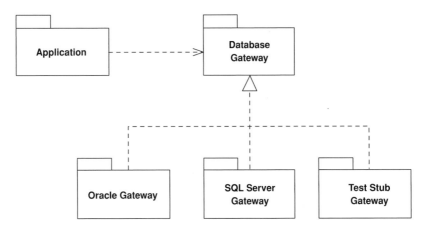

Figure 7.4 *A package implemented by other packages*

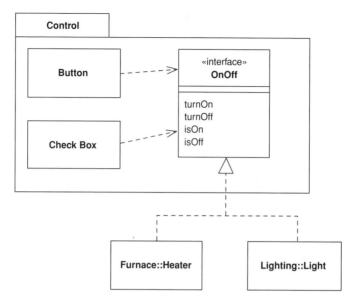

Figure 7.5 *Defining a required interface in a client package*

When to Use Package Diagrams

I find package diagrams extremely useful on larger-scale systems to get a picture of the dependencies between major elements of a system. These diagrams correspond well to common programming structures. Plotting diagrams of packages and dependencies helps you keep an application's dependencies under control.

Package diagrams represent a compile-time grouping mechanism. For showing how objects are composed at runtime, use a composite structure diagram (page 135).

Where to Find Out More

The best discussion I know of packages and how to use them is [Martin]. Robert Martin has long had an almost pathological obsession with dependencies and writes well about how to pay attention to dependencies so that you can control and minimize them.

Chapter 8

Deployment Diagrams

Deployment diagrams show a system's physical layout, revealing which pieces of software run on what pieces of hardware. Deployment diagrams are really very simple; hence the short chapter.

Figure 8.1 is a simple example of a deployment diagram. The main items on the diagram are nodes connected by communication paths. A **node** is something that can host some software. Nodes come in two forms. A **device** is hardware, it may be a computer or a simpler piece of hardware connected to a system. An **execution environment** is software that itself hosts or contains other software, examples are an operating system or a container process.

The nodes contain **artifacts**, which are the physical manifestations of software: usually, files. These files might be executables (such as .exe files, binaries, DLLs, JAR files, assemblies, or scripts), or data files, configuration files, HTML documents, and so on. Listing an artifact within a node shows that the artifact is deployed to that node in the running system.

You can show artifacts either as class boxes or by listing the name within a node. If you show them as class boxes, you can add a document icon or the «artifact» keyword. You can tag nodes or artifacts with tagged values to indicate various interesting information about the node, such as vendor, operating system, location, or anything else that takes your fancy.

Often, you'll have multiple physical nodes carrying out the same logical task. You can either show this with multiple node boxes or state the number as a tagged value. In Figure 8.1, I used the tag number deployed to indicate three physical Web servers, but there's no standard tag for this.

Artifacts are often the implementation of a component. To show this, you can use a tagged value in the artifact box.

Communication paths between nodes indicate how things communicate. You can label these paths with information about the communication protocols that are used.

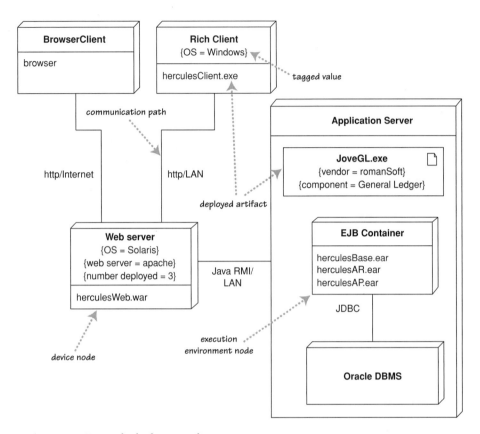

Figure 8.1 *Example deployment diagram*

When to Use Deployment Diagrams

Don't let the brevity of this chapter make you think that deployment diagrams shouldn't be used. They are very handy in showing what is deployed where, so any nontrivial deployment can make good use of them.

Chapter 9

Use Cases

Use cases are a technique for capturing the functional requirements of a system. Use cases work by describing the typical interactions between the users of a system and the system itself, providing a narrative of how a system is used.

Rather than describe use cases head-on, I find it easier to sneak up on them from behind and start by describing scenarios. A **scenario** is a sequence of steps describing an interaction between a user and a system. So if we have a Web-based on-line store, we might have a Buy a Product scenario that would say this:

> *The customer browses the catalog and adds desired items to the shopping basket. When the customer wishes to pay, the customer describes the shipping and credit card information and confirms the sale. The system checks the authorization on the credit card and confirms the sale both immediately and with a follow-up e-mail.*

This scenario is one thing that can happen. However, the credit card authorization might fail, and this would be a separate scenario. In another case, you may have a regular customer for whom you don't need to capture the shipping and credit card information, and this is a third scenario.

All these scenarios are different yet similar. The essence of their similarity is that in all these three scenarios, the user has the same goal: to buy a product. The user doesn't always succeed, but the goal remains. This user goal is the key to use cases: A **use case** is a set of scenarios tied together by a common user goal.

In use case–speak, the users are referred to as actors. An **actor** is a role that a user plays with respect to the system. Actors might include customer, customer service rep, sales manager, and product analyst. Actors carry out use cases. A single actor may perform many use cases; conversely, a use case may have several actors performing it. Usually, you have many customers, so many people can be the customer actor. Also, one person may act as more than one actor, such as a sales manager who does customer service rep tasks. An actor doesn't have to be human. If the system performs a service for another computer system, that other system is an actor.

Actor isn't really the right term; *role* would be much better. Apparently, there was a mistranslation from Swedish, and *actor* is the term the use case community uses.

Use cases are well known as an important part of the UML. However, the surprise is that in many ways, the definition of use cases in the UML is rather sparse. Nothing in the UML describes how you should capture the content of a use case. What the UML describes is a use case diagram, which shows how use cases relate to each other. But almost all the value of use cases lies in the content, and the diagram is of rather limited value.

Content of a Use Case

There is no standard way to write the content of a use case, and different formats work well in different cases. Figure 9.1 shows a common style to use. You begin by picking one of the scenarios as the **main success scenario.** You start the body of the use case by writing the main success scenario as a sequence of numbered steps. You then take the other scenarios and write them as **extensions,** describing them in terms of variations on the main success scenario. Extensions can be successes—user achieves the goal, as in 3a—or failures, as in 6a.

Each use case has a primary actor, which calls on the system to deliver a service. The primary actor is the actor with the goal the use case is trying to satisfy and is usually, but not always, the initiator of the use case. There may be other actors as well with which the system communicates while carrying out the use case. These are known as secondary actors.

Each step in a use case is an element of the interaction between an actor and the system. Each step should be a simple statement and should clearly show who is carrying out the step. The step should show the intent of the actor, not the mechanics of what the actor does. Consequently, you don't describe the user interface in the use case. Indeed, writing the use case usually precedes designing the user interface.

An extension within the use case names a condition that results in different interactions from those described in the main success scenario (MSS) and states what those differences are. Start the extension by naming the step at which the condition is detected and provide a short description of the condition. Follow the condition with numbered steps in the same style as the main success scenario.

Buy a Product

Goal Level: Sea Level

Main Success Scenario:
1. Customer browses catalog and selects items to buy
2. Customer goes to check out
3. Customer fills in shipping information (address; next-day or 3-day delivery)
4. System presents full pricing information, including shipping
5. Customer fills in credit card information
6. System authorizes purchase
7. System confirms sale immediately
8. System sends confirming e-mail to customer

Extensions:
3a: Customer is regular customer
    .1: System displays current shipping, pricing, and billing information
    .2: Customer may accept or override these defaults, returns to MSS at step 6
6a: System fails to authorize credit purchase
    .1: Customer may reenter credit card information or may cancel

---

Figure 9.1 *Example use case text*

Finish these steps by describing where you return to the main success scenario, if you do.

The use case structure is a great way to brainstorm alternatives to the main success scenario. For each step, ask, How could this go differently? and in particular, What could go wrong? It's usually best to brainstorm all the extension conditions first, before you get bogged down working out the consequences. You'll probably think of more conditions this way, which translates to fewer goofs that you have to pick up later.

A complicated step in a use case can be another use case. In UML terms, we say that the first use case **includes** the second. There's no standard way to show an included use case in the text, but I find that underlining, which suggests a hyperlink, works very nicely and in many tools really will be a hyperlink. Thus in Figure 9.1, the first step includes the use case "browse catalog and select items to buy."

Included use cases can be useful for a complex step that would clutter the main scenario or for steps that are repeated in several use cases. However, don't try to break down use cases into sub–use cases and subsub–use cases using functional decomposition. Such a decomposition is a good way to waste a lot of time.

As well as the steps in the scenarios, you can add some other common information to a use case.

- A **pre-condition** describes what the system should ensure is true before the system allows the use case to begin. This is useful for telling the programmers what conditions they don't have to check for in their code.

- A **guarantee** describes what the system will ensure at the end of the use case. Success guarantees hold after a successful scenario; minimal guarantees hold after any scenario.

- A **trigger** specifies the event that gets the use case started.

When you're considering adding elements, be skeptical. It's better to do too little than too much. Also, work hard to keep the use case brief and easy to read. I've found that long, detailed use cases don't get read, which rather defeats the purpose.

The amount of detail you need in a use case depends on the amount of risk in that use case. Often, you need details on only a few key use cases early on; others can be fleshed out just before you implement them. You don't have to write all the detail down; verbal communication is often very effective, particularly within an iterative cycle in which needs are quickly met by running code.

Use Case Diagrams

As I said earlier, the UML is silent on the content of a use case but does provide a diagram format for showing them, as in Figure 9.2. Although the diagram is sometimes useful, it isn't mandatory. In your use case work, don't put too much effort into the diagram. Instead, concentrate on the textual content of the use cases.

The best way to think of a use case diagram is that it's a graphical table of contents for the use case set. It's also similar to the context diagram used in structured methods, as it shows the system boundary and the interactions with the outside world. The use case diagram shows the actors, the use cases, and the relationships between them:

- Which actors carry out which use cases

- Which use cases include other use cases

The UML includes other relationships between use cases beyond the simple includes, such as «extend». I strongly suggest that you ignore them. I've seen too

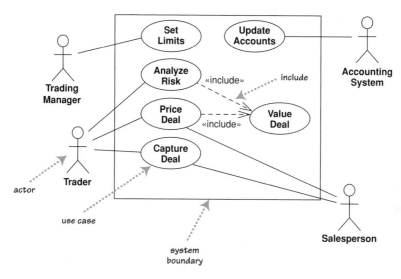

Figure 9.2 *Use case diagram*

many situations in which teams can get terribly hung up on when to use different use case relationships, and such energy is wasted. Instead, concentrate on the textual description of a use case; that's where the real value of the technique lies.

Levels of Use Cases

A common problem with use cases is that by focusing on the interaction between a user and the system, you can neglect situations in which a change to a business process may be the best way to deal with the problem. Often, you hear people talk about system use cases and business use cases. The terms are not precise, but in general, a **system use case** is an interaction with the software, whereas a **business use case** discusses how a business responds to a customer or an event.

[Cockburn, use cases] suggests a scheme of levels of use cases. The core use cases are at "sea level." **Sea-level** use cases typically represent a discrete interaction between a primary actor and the system. Such use cases will deliver something of value to the primary actor and usually take from a couple of minutes to half an hour for the primary actor to complete. Use cases that are there only because they are included by sea-level use cases are **fish level**. Higher, **kite-level** use cases show how the sea-level use cases fit into wider business interactions. Kite-level use cases are usually business use cases, whereas sea and fish levels are system use cases. You should have most of your use cases at the sea level. I prefer to indicate the level at the top of the use case, as in Figure 9.1.

Use Cases and Features (or Stories)

Many approaches use features of a system—Extreme Programming calls them user stories—to help describe requirements. A common question is how features and use cases interrelate.

Features are a good way of chunking up a system for planning an iterative project, whereby each iteration delivers a number of features. Use cases provide a narrative of how the actors use the system. Hence, although both techniques describe requirements, their purposes are different.

Although you can go directly to describing features, many people find it helpful to develop use cases first and then generate a list of features. A feature may be a whole use case, a scenario in a use case, a step in a use case, or some variant behavior, such as adding yet another depreciation method for your asset valuations, that doesn't show up in a use case narrative. Usually, features end up being more fine grained than use cases.

When to Use Use Cases

Use cases are a valuable tool to help understand the functional requirements of a system. A first pass at use cases should be made early on. More detailed versions of use cases should be worked just prior to developing that use case.

It is important to remember that use cases represent an *external* view of the system. As such, don't expect any correlations between use cases and the classes inside the system.

The more I see of use cases, the less valuable the use case diagram seems to be. With use cases, concentrate your energy on their text rather than on the diagram. Despite the fact that the UML has nothing to say about the use case text, it is the text that contains all the value in the technique.

A big danger of use cases is that people make them too complicated and get stuck. Usually, you'll get less hurt by doing too little than by doing too much. A couple of pages per use case is just fine for most cases. If you have too little, at least you'll have a short, readable document that's a starting point for questions. If you have too much, hardly anyone will read and understand it.

Where to Find Out More

Use cases were originally popularized by Ivar Jacobson in [Jacobson, OOSE].

Although use cases have been around for a while, there's been little standardization on their use. The UML is silent on the important contents of a use case and has standardized only the much less important diagrams. As a result, you can find a divergent range of opinions on use cases.

In the last few years, however, [Cockburn, use cases] has become the standard book on the subject. In this chapter, I've followed the terminology and advice of that book for the excellent reason that when we've disagreed in the past, I've usually ended up agreeing with Alistair Cockburn in the end. He also maintains a Web site at **http://usecases.org.** [Constantine and Lockwood] provides a convincing process for deriving user interfaces from use cases; also see **http://foruse.com.**

Chapter 10

State Machine Diagrams

State machine diagrams are a familiar technique to describe the behavior of a system. Various forms of state diagrams have been around since the 1960s and the earliest object-oriented techniques adopted them to show behavior. In object-oriented approaches, you draw a state machine diagram for a single class to show the lifetime behavior of a single object.

Whenever people write about state machines, the examples are inevitably cruise controls or vending machines. As I'm a little bored with them, I decided to use a controller for a secret panel in a Gothic castle. In this castle, I want to keep my valuables in a safe that's hard to find. So to reveal the lock to the safe, I have to remove a strategic candle from its holder, but this will reveal the lock only while the door is closed. Once I can see the lock, I can insert my key to open the safe. For extra safety, I make sure that I can open the safe only if I replace the candle first. If a thief neglects this precaution, I'll unleash a nasty monster to devour him.

Figure 10.1 shows a state machine diagram of the controller class that directs my unusual security system. The state diagram starts with the state of the controller object when it's created: in Figure 10.1, the Wait state. The diagram indicates this with **initial pseudostate**, which is not a state but has an arrow that points to the initial state.

The diagram shows that the controller can be in three states: Wait, Lock, and Open. The diagram also gives the rules by which the controller changes from state to state. These rules are in the form of transitions: the lines that connect the states.

The **transition** indicates a movement from one state to another. Each transition has a label that comes in three parts: `trigger-signature [guard]/activity`. All the parts are optional. The `trigger-signature` is usually a single event that triggers a potential change of state. The `guard`, if present, is a Boolean condition that must be true for the transition to be taken. The activity is some behavior that's executed during the transition. It may be any behavioral expression. The full form of a `trigger-signature`

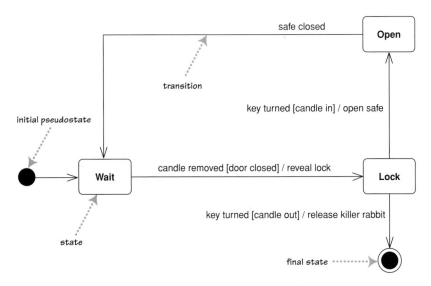

Figure 10.1 *A simple state machine diagram*

may include multiple events and parameters. So in Figure 10.1, you read the outward transition from the Wait state as "In the Wait state if the candle is removed providing the door is closed, you reveal the lock and move to the Lock state."

All three parts to a transition are optional. A missing activity indicates that you don't do anything during the transition. A missing guard indicates that you always take the transition if the event occurs. A missing trigger-signature is rare but does occur. It indicates that you take the transition immediately, which you see mostly with activity states, which I'll come to in a moment.

When an event occurs in a state, you can take only one transition out of it. So if you use multiple transitions with the same event, as in the Lock state of Figure 10.1, the guards must be mutually exclusive. If an event occurs and no transition is valid—for example, a safe-closed event in the Wait state or a candle-removed event with the door open—the event is ignored.

The final state indicates that the state machine is completed, implying the deletion of the controller object. Thus, if someone should be so careless as to fall for my trap, the controller object terminates, so I would need to put the rabbit in its cage, mop the floor, and reboot the system.

Remember that state machines can show only what the object directly observes or activates. So although you might expect me to add or remove things from the safe when it's open, I don't put that on the state diagram, because the controller cannot tell.

When developers talk about objects, they often refer to the state of the objects to mean the combination of all the data in the fields of the objects. However, the state in a state machine diagram is a more abstract notion of state; essentially, different states imply a different way of reacting to events.

Internal Activities

States can react to events without transition, using **internal activities:** putting the event, guard, and activity inside the state box itself.

Figure 10.2 shows a state with internal activities of the character and help events, as you might find on a UI text field. An internal activity is similar to a **self-transition:** a transition that loops back to the same state. The syntax for internal activities follows the same logic for event, guard, and procedure.

Figure 10.2 also shows two special activities: the entry and exit activities. The **entry activity** is executed whenever you enter a state; the **exit activity,** whenever you leave. However, internal activities do not trigger the entry and exit activities; that is the difference between internal activities and self-transitions.

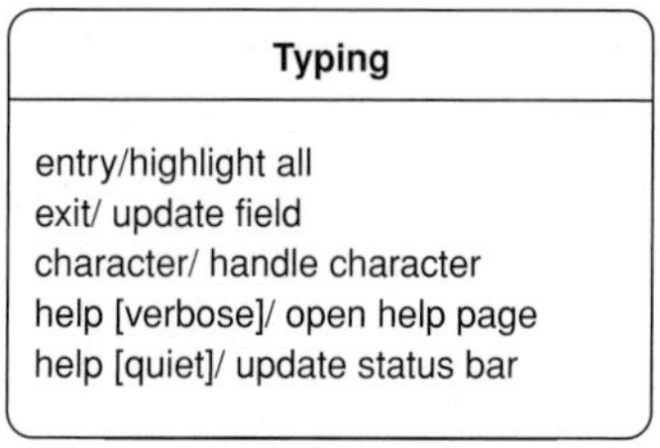

Typing

entry/highlight all
exit/ update field
character/ handle character
help [verbose]/ open help page
help [quiet]/ update status bar

Figure 10.2 *Internal events shown with the typing state of a text field*

Activity States

In the states I've described so far, the object is quiet and waiting for the next event before it does something. However, you can have states in which the object is doing some ongoing work.

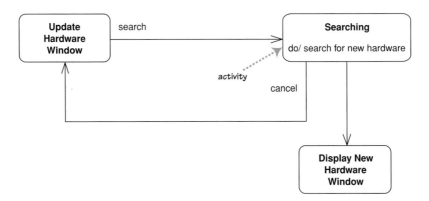

Figure 10.3 *A state with an activity*

The Searching state in Figure 10.3 is such an **activity state:** The ongoing activity is marked with the do/; hence the term **do-activity.** Once the search is completed, any transitions without an event, such as the one to display new hardware, are taken. If the cancel event occurs during the activity, the do-activity is unceremoniously halted, and we go back to the Update Hardware Window state.

Both do-activities and regular activities represent carrying out some behavior. The critical difference between the two is that regular activities occur "instantaneously" and cannot be interrupted by regular events, while do-activities can take finite time and can be interrupted, as in Figure 10.3. Instantaneous will mean different things for different system; for hard real-time systems, it might be a few machine instructions, but for desktop software might be several seconds.

UML 1 used the term **action** for regular activities and used activity only for do-activities.

Superstates

Often, you'll find that several states share common transitions and internal activities. In these cases, you can make them substates and move the shared behavior into a superstate, as in Figure 10.4. Without the superstate, you would have to draw a cancel transition for all three states within the Enter Connection Details state.

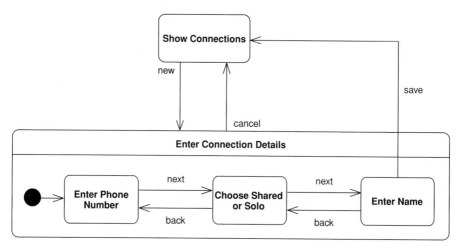

Figure 10.4 *Superstate with nested substates*

Concurrent States

States can be broken into several orthogonal state diagrams that run concurrently. Figure 10.5 shows a pathetically simple alarm clock that can play either CDs or the radio and show either the current time or the alarm time.

The choices CD/radio and current/alarm time are orthogonal choices. If you wanted to represent this with a nonorthogonal state diagram, you would need a messy diagram that would get very much out of hand should you want more states. Separating out the two areas of behavior into separate state diagrams makes it much clearer.

Figure 10.5 also includes a **history pseudostate**. This indicates that when the clock is switched on, the radio/CD choice goes back to the state the clock was in when it was turned off. The arrow from the history pseudostate indicates what state to be in on the first time when there is no history.

Implementing State Diagrams

A state diagram can be implemented in three main ways: nested switch, the State pattern, and state tables. The most direct approach to handling a state

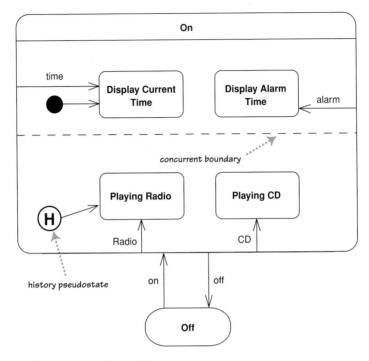

Figure 10.5 *Concurrent orthogonal states*

diagram is a nested switch statement, such as Figure 10.6. Although it's direct, it's long-winded, even for this simple case. It's also very easy for this approach to get out of control, so I don't like using it even for simple cases.

The **State pattern** [Gang of Four] creates a hierarchy of state classes to handle behavior of the states. Each state in the diagram has one state subclass. The controller has methods for each event, which simply forwards to the state class. The state diagram of Figure 10.1 would yield an implementation indicated by the classes of Figure 10.7.

The top of the hierarchy is an abstract class that implements all the event-handling methods to do nothing. For each concrete state, you simply override the specific event methods for which that state has transitions.

The **state table** approach captures the state diagram information as data. So Figure 10.1 might end up represented in a table like Table 10.1. We then build either an interpreter that uses the state table at runtime or a code generator that generates classes based on the state table.

Obviously, the state table is more work to do once, but then you can use it every time you have a state problem to hold. A runtime state table can also be

```csharp
public void HandleEvent (PanelEvent anEvent) {
  switch (CurrentState) {
    case PanelState.Open :
      switch (anEvent) {
        case PanelEvent.SafeClosed :
          CurrentState = PanelState.Wait;
          break;
      }
      break;
    case PanelState.Wait :
      switch (anEvent) {
        case PanelEvent.CandleRemoved :
          if (isDoorClosed) {
            RevealLock();
            CurrentState = PanelState.Lock;
          }
          break;
      }
      break;
    case PanelState.Lock :
      switch (anEvent) {
        case PanelEvent.KeyTurned :
          if (isCandleIn) {
            OpenSafe();
            CurrentState = PanelState.Open;
          } else {
            ReleaseKillerRabbit();
            CurrentState = PanelState.Final;
          }
          break;
      }
      break;
  }
}
```

Figure 10.6 *A C# nested switch to handle the state transition from Figure 10.1*

modified without recompilation, which in some contexts is quite handy. The state pattern is easier to put together when you need it, and although it needs a new class for each state, it's a small amount of code to write in each case.

These implementations are pretty minimal, but they should give you an idea of how to go about implementing state diagrams. In each case, implementing state models leads to very boilerplate code, so it's usually best to use some form of code generation to do it.

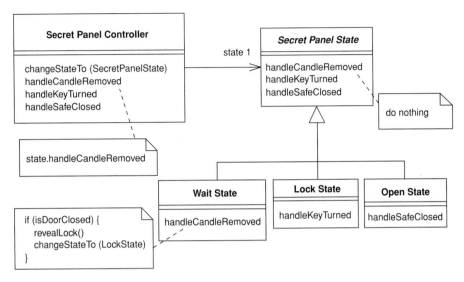

Figure 10.7 *A State pattern implementation for Figure 10.1*

Table 10.1 *A State Table for Figure 10.1*

Source State	Target State	Event	Guard	Procedure
Wait	Lock	Candle removed	Door closed	Reveal lock
Lock	Open	Key turned	Candle in	Open safe
Lock	Final	Key turned	Candle out	Release killer rabbit
Open	Wait	Safe closed		

When to Use State Diagrams

State diagrams are good at describing the behavior of an object across several use cases. State diagrams are not very good at describing behavior that involves a number of objects collaborating. As such, it is useful to combine state diagrams with other techniques. For instance, interaction diagrams (see Chapter 4) are good at describing the behavior of several objects in a single use case, and activity diagrams (see Chapter 11) are good at showing the general sequence of activities for several objects and use cases.

Not everyone finds state diagrams natural. Keep an eye on how people are working with them. It may be that your team does not find state diagrams useful to its way of working. That is not a big problem; as always, you should remember to use the mix of techniques that works for you.

If you do use state diagrams, don't try to draw them for every class in the system. Although this approach is often used by high-ceremony completists, it is almost always a waste of effort. Use state diagrams only for those classes that exhibit interesting behavior, where building the state diagram helps you understand what is going on. Many people find that UI and control objects have the kind of behavior that is useful to depict with a state diagram.

Where to Find Out More

Both the *User Guide* [Booch, UML user] and the *Reference Manual* [Rumbaugh, UML Reference] have more information on state diagrams. Real-time designers tend to use state models a lot, so it's no surprise that [Douglass]) has a lot to say about state diagrams, including information on how to implement them. [Martin] contains a very good chapter on the various ways of implementing state diagrams.

Chapter 11

Activity Diagrams

Activity diagrams are a technique to describe procedural logic, business process, and work flow. In many ways, they play a role similar to flowcharts, but the principal difference between them and flowchart notation is that they support parallel behavior.

Activity diagrams have seen some of the biggest changes over the versions of the UML, so they have, not surprisingly, been significantly extended and altered again for UML 2. In UML 1, activity diagrams were seen as special cases of state diagrams. This caused a lot of problems for people modeling work flows, which activity diagrams are well suited for. In UML 2, that tie was removed.

Figure 11.1 shows a simple example of an activity diagram. We begin at the **initial node** action and then do the action Receive Order. Once that is done, we encounter a fork. A **fork** has one incoming flow and several outgoing concurrent flows.

Figure 11.1 says that Fill Order, Send Invoice, and the subsequent actions occur in parallel. Essentially, this means that the sequence between them is irrelevant. I could fill the order, send the invoice, deliver, and then receive payment; or, I could send the invoice, receive the payment, fill the order, and then deliver: You get the picture.

I can also do these actions by interleaving. I grab the first line item from stores, type up the invoice, grab the second line item, put the invoice in an envelope, and so forth. Or, I could do some of this simultaneously: type up the invoice with one hand while I reach into my stores with another. Any of these sequences is correct, according to the diagram.

The activity diagram allows whoever is doing the process to choose the order in which to do things. In other words, the diagram merely states the essential sequencing rules I have to follow. This is important for business modeling

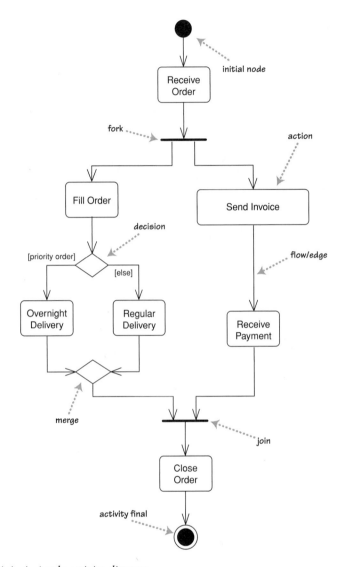

Figure 11.1 *A simple activity diagram*

because processes often occur in parallel. It's also useful for concurrent algorithms, in which independent threads can do things in parallel.

When you have parallelism, you'll need to synchronize. We don't close the
order until it is delivered and paid for. We show this with the **join** before the Close
Order action. With a join, the outgoing flow is taken only when all the incom-

ing flows reach the join. So you can close the order only when you have both received the payment and delivered.

UML 1 had particular rules for balancing the forks and joins, as activity diagrams were special cases of state diagrams. With UML 2, such balancing is no longer needed.

You'll notice that the nodes on an activity diagram are called actions, not activities. Strictly, an activity refers to a sequence of actions, so the diagram shows an activity that's made up of actions.

Conditional behavior is delineated by decisions and merges. A **decision,** called *branch* in UML 1, has a single incoming flow and several guarded outbound flows. Each outbound flow has a guard: a Boolean condition placed inside square brackets. Each time you reach a decision, you can take only one of the outbound flows, so the guards should be mutually exclusive. Using [else] as a guard indicates that the [else] flow should be used if all the other guards on the decision are false.

In Figure 11.1, after an order is filled, there is a decision. If you have a rush order, you do an Overnight Delivery; otherwise, you do a Regular Delivery.

A **merge** has multiple input flows and a single output. A merge marks the end of conditional behavior started by a decision.

In my diagrams, each action has a single flow coming in and a single flow going out. In UML 1, multiple incoming flows had an implicit merge. That is, your action would execute if any flow triggered. In UML 2, this has changed so there's an implicit join instead; thus, the action executes only if all flows trigger. As a result of this change, I recommend that you use only a single incoming and outgoing flow to an action and show all joins and merges explicitly; that will avoid confusion.

Decomposing an Action

Actions can be decomposed into subactivities. I can take the delivery logic of Figure 11.1 and define it as its own activity (Figure 11.2). Then I can call it as an action (Figure 11.3 on page 121).

Actions can be implemented either as subactivities or as methods on classes. You can show a subactivity by using the rake symbol. You can show a call on a method with syntax class-name::method-name. You can also write a code fragment into the action symbol if the invoked behavior isn't a single method call.

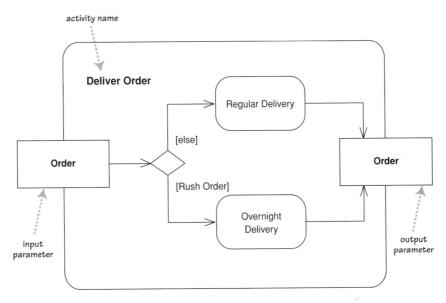

Figure 11.2 *A subsidiary activity diagram*

Partitions

Activity diagrams tell you what happens, but they do not tell you who does what. In programming, this means that the diagram does not convey which class is responsible for each action. In business process modeling, this does not convey which part of an organization carries out which action. This isn't necessarily a problem; often, it makes sense to concentrate on what gets done rather than on who does what parts of the behavior.

If you want to show who does what, you can divide an activity diagram into **partitions,** which show which actions one class or organization unit carries out. Figure 11.4 (on page 122) shows a simple example of this, showing how the actions involved in order processing can be separated among various departments.

The partitioning of Figure 11.4 is a simple one-dimensional partitioning. This style is often referred to as **swim lanes,** for obvious reasons and was the only form used in UML 1.x. In UML 2, you can use a two-dimensional grid, so the swimming metaphor no longer holds water. You can also take each dimension and divide the rows or columns hierarchically.

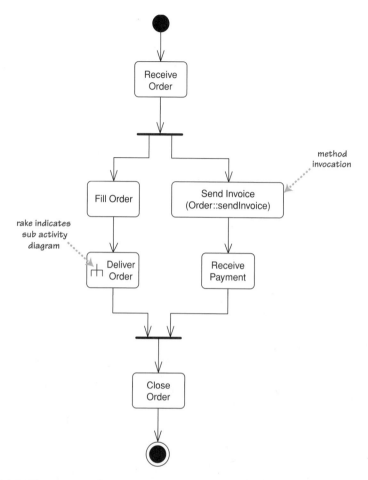

Figure 11.3 *The activity of Figure 11.1 modified to invoke the activity in Figure 11.2*

Signals

In the simple example of Figure 11.1, activity diagrams have a clearly defined start point, which corresponds to an invocation of a program or routine. Actions can also respond to signals.

A **time signal** occurs because of the passage of time. Such signals might indicate the end of a month in a financial period or each microsecond in a real-time controller.

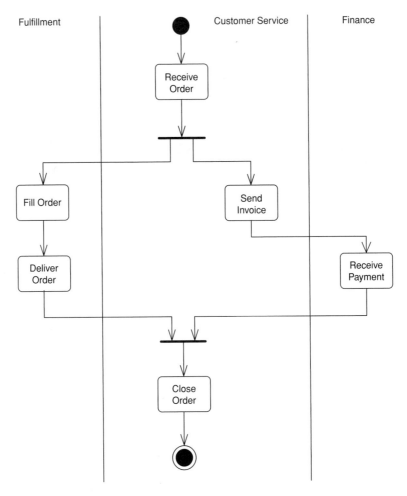

Figure 11.4 *Partitions on an activity diagram*

Figure 11.5 shows an activity that listens for two signals. A **signal** indicates that the activity receives an event from an outside process. This indicates that the activity constantly listens for those signals, and the diagram defines how the activity reacts.

In the case of Figure 11.5, 2 hours before my flight leaves, I need to start packing my bags. If I'm quick to pack them, I still cannot leave until the taxi arrives. If the taxi arrives before my bags are packed, it has to wait for me to finish before we go.

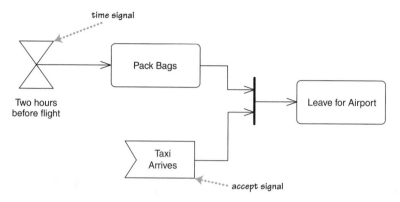

Figure 11.5 *Signals on an activity diagram*

As well as accepting signals, we can send them. This is useful when we have to send a message and then wait for a reply before we can continue. Figure 11.6 shows a good example of this with a common idiom of timing out. Note that the two flows are in a race: The first to reach the final state will win and terminate the other flow. I'm using a single activity final here. This means the same as two separate icons (i.e., there's no implicit join for activity finals).

Although accepts are usually just waiting for an external event, we can also show a flow going into them. That indicates that we don't start listening until the flow triggers the accept.

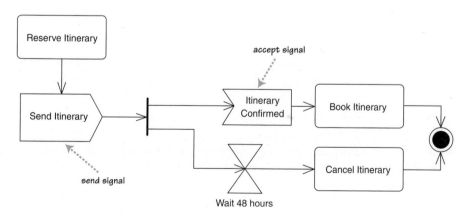

Figure 11.6 *Sending and receiving signals*

Tokens

If you're sufficiently brave to venture into the demonic depths of the UML specification, you'll find that the activity section of the specification talks a lot about tokens and their production and consumption. The initial node creates a token, which then passes to the next action, which executes and then passes the token to the next. At a fork, one token comes in, and the fork produces a token on each of its outward flows. Conversely, on a join, as each inbound token arrives, nothing happens until all the tokens appear at the join; then a token is produced on the outward flow.

You can visualize the tokens with coins or counters moving across the diagram. As you get to more complicated examples of activity diagrams, tokens often make it easier to visualize things.

Flows and Edges

UML 2 uses the terms **flow** and **edge** synonymously to describe the connections between two actions. The simplest kind of edge is the simple arrow between two actions. You can give an edge a name if you like, but most of the time, a simple arrow will suffice.

If you're having difficulty routing lines, you can use connectors, which simply save you having to draw a line the whole distance. When you use connectors, you must use them in pairs: one with incoming flow, one with an outgoing flow, and both with the same label. I tend to avoid using connectors if at all possible, as they break up the visualization of the flow of control.

The simplest edges pass a token that has no meaning other than to control the flow. However, you can also pass objects along edges; the objects then play the role of tokens, as well as carry data. If you are passing an object along the edge, you can show that by putting a class box on the edge, or you can use pins on the actions, although pins imply some more subtleties that I'll describe shortly.

All the styles shown in Figure 11.7 are equivalent; you should use whichever conveys best what you are trying to communicate. Most of the time, the simple arrow is quite enough.

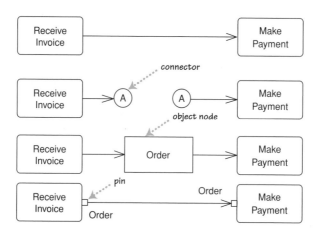

Figure 11.7 *Four ways of showing an edge*

Pins and Transformations

Actions can have parameters, just as methods do. You don't need to show information about parameters on the activity diagram, but if you wish, you can show them with **pins**. If you're decomposing an action, pins correspond to the parameter boxes on the decomposed diagram.

When you're drawing an activity diagram strictly, you have to ensure that the output parameters of an outbound action match the input parameters of another. If they don't match, you can indicate a **transformation** (Figure 11.8) to get from one to another. The transformation must be an expression that's free of side effects: essentially, a query on the output pin parameter that supplies an object of the right type for the input pin.

You don't have to show pins on an activity diagram. Pins are best when you want to look at the data needed and produced by the various actions. In business process modeling, you can use pins to show the resources produced and consumed by actions.

If you use pins, it's safe to show multiple flows coming into the same action. The pin notation reinforces the implicit join, and UML 1 didn't have pins, so there's no confusion with the earlier assumptions.

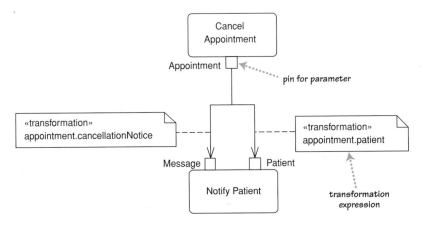

Figure 11.8 *Transformation on a flow*

Expansion Regions

With activity diagrams, you often run into situations in which one action's output triggers multiple invocations of another action. There are several ways to show this, but the best way is to use an expansion region. An **expansion region** marks an activity diagram area where actions occur once for each item in a collection.

In Figure 11.9, the Choose Topics action generates a list of topics as its output. Each element of this list then becomes a token for input to the Write Article action. Similarly, each Review Article action generates a single article that's added to the output list of the expansion region. When all the tokens in the expansion region end up in the output collection, the region generates a single token for the list that's passed to Publish Newsletter.

In this case, you have the same number of items in the output collection as you do in the input collection. However, you may have fewer, in which case the expansion region acts as a filter.

In Figure 11.9, all the articles are written and reviewed in parallel, which is marked by the «concurrent» keyword. You can also have an iterative expansion region. Iterative regions must fully process each input element one at a time.

If you have only a single action that needs multiple invocation, you use the shorthand of Figure 11.10. The shorthand assumes concurrent expansion, as

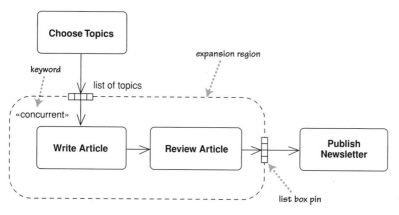

Figure 11.9 *Expansion region*

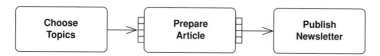

Figure 11.10 *Shorthand for a single action in an expansion region*

that's the most common. This notation corresponds to the UML 1 concept of dynamic concurrency.

Flow Final

Once you get multiple tokens, as in an expansion region, you often get flows that stop even when the activity as a whole doesn't end. A **flow final** indicates the end of one particular flow, without terminating the whole activity.

Figure 11.11 shows this by modifying the example of Figure 11.9 to allow articles to be rejected. If an article is rejected, the token is destroyed by the flow final. Unlike an activity final, the rest of the activity can continue. This approach allows expansion regions to act as filters, whereby the output collection is smaller than the input collection.

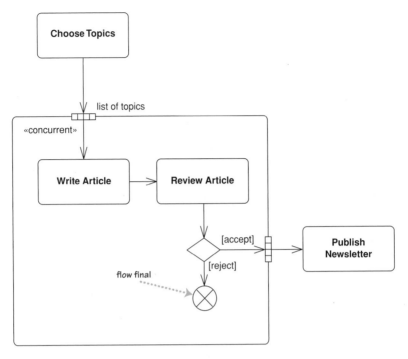

Figure 11.11 *Flow finals in an activity*

Join Specifications

By default, a join lets execution pass on its outward flow when all its input flows have arrived at the join. (Or in more formal speak, it emits a token on its output flow when a token has arrived on each input flow.) In some cases, particularly when you have a flow with multiple tokens, it's useful to have a more involved rule.

A **join specification** is a Boolean expression attached to a join. Each time a token arrives at the join, the join specification is evaluated and if true, an output token is emitted. So in Figure 11.12, whenever I select a drink or insert a coin, the machine evaluates the join specification. The machine slakes my thirst only if I've put in enough money. If, as in this case, you want to indicate that you have received a token on each input flow, you label the flows and include them in the join specification.

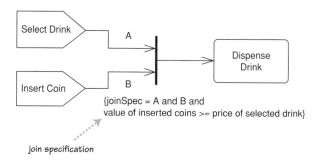

Figure 11.12 *Join specification*

And There's More

I should stress that this chapter only scratches the surface on activity diagrams. As with so much of the UML, you could write a whole book on this one technique alone. Indeed, I think that activity diagrams would make a very suitable topic for a book that really dug into the notation and how to use it.

The vital question is how widely they get used. Activity diagrams aren't the most widely used UML technique at the moment, and their flow-modeling progenitors weren't very popular either. Diagrammatic techniques haven't yet caught on much for describing behavior in this kind of way. On the other hand, there are signs in a number of communities of a pent-up demand that a standard technique will help to satisfy.

When to Use Activity Diagrams

The great strength of activity diagrams lies in the fact that they support and encourage parallel behavior. This makes them a great tool for work flow and process modeling, and indeed much of the push in UML 2 has come from people involved in work flow.

You can also use an activity diagram as a UML-compliant flowchart. Although this allows you to do flowcharts in a way that sticks with the UML, it's hardly very exciting. In principle, you can take advantages of the forks and joins to describe parallel algorithms for concurrent programs. Although I don't travel in concurrent circles that much, I haven't seen much evidence of people using them there. I think the reason is that most of the complexity of concurrent programming is in avoiding contention on data, and activity diagrams don't help much with that.

The main strength of doing this may come with people using UML as a programming language. In this case, activity diagrams represent an important technique to represent behavioral logic.

I've often seen activity diagrams used to describe a use case. The danger of this approach is that often, domain experts don't follow them easily. If so, you'd be better off with the usual textual form.

Where to Find Out More

Although activity diagrams have always been rather complicated and are even more so with UML 2, there hasn't been a good book that describes them in depth. I hope this gap will get filled someday.

Various flow-oriented techniques are similar in style to activity diagrams. One of the better known—but hardly well known—is Petri Nets, for which **http://www.daimi.au.dk/PetriNets/** is a good Web site.

Chapter 12

Communication Diagrams

Communication diagrams, a kind of interaction diagram, emphasize the data links between the various participants in the interaction. Instead of drawing each participant as a lifeline and showing the sequence of messages by vertical direction as the sequence diagram does, the communication diagram allows free placement of participants, allows you to draw links to show how the participants connect, and use numbering to show the sequence of messages.

In UML 1.x, these diagrams were called **collaboration diagrams**. This name stuck well, and I suspect that it will be a while before people get used to the new name. (These are different from Collaborations [page 143]; hence the name change.)

Figure 12.1 shows a communication diagram for the same centralized control interaction as in Figure 4.1. With a communication diagram, we can show how the participants are linked together.

As well as showing links that are instances of associations, we can also show transient links, which arise only the context of the interaction. In this case, the «local» link from Order to Product is a local variable; other transient links are «parameter» and «global». These keywords were used in UML 1 but are missing from UML 2. Because they are useful, I expect them to stay around in conventional use.

The numbering style of Figure 12.1 is straightforward and commonly used, but actually isn't legal UML. To be kosher UML, you have to use a nested decimal numbering scheme, as in Figure 12.2.

The reason for the nested decimal numbers is to resolve ambiguity with self-calls. In Figure 4.1, you can clearly see that getDiscountInfo is called within the method calculateDiscount. With the flat numbering of Figure 12.1, however, you can't tell whether getDiscountInfo is called within calculateDiscount or within the overall calculatePrice method. The nested numbering scheme resolves this problem.

Despite its illegality, many people prefer a flat numbering scheme. The nested numbers can get very tangled, particularly as calls get rather nested, leading to

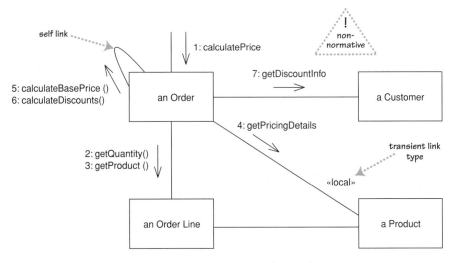

Figure 12.1 *Communication diagram for centralized control*

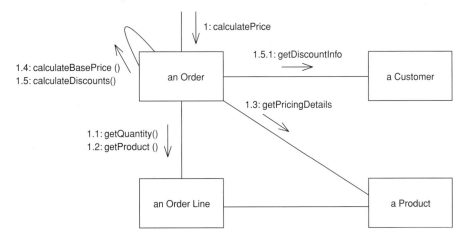

Figure 12.2 *Communication diagram with nested decimal numbering*

such sequence numbers as 1.1.1.2.1.1. In these cases, the cure for ambiguity can be worse than the disease.

As well as numbers, you may also see letters on messages; these letters indicate different threads of control. So messages A5 and B2 would be in different threads; messages 1a1 and 1b1 would be different threads concurrently nested within message 1. You also see thread letters on sequence diagrams, although this doesn't convey the concurrency visually.

Communication diagrams don't have any precise notation for control logic. They do allow you to use iteration markers and guards (page 59), but they don't allow you to fully specify control logic. There is no special notation for creating or deleting objects, but the «create» and «delete» keywords are common conventions.

When to Use Communication Diagrams

The main question with communication diagrams is when to use them rather than the more common sequence diagrams. A strong part of the decision is personal preference: Some people like one over the other. Often, that drives the choice more than anything else. On the whole, most people seem to prefer sequence diagrams, and for once, I'm with the majority.

A more rational approach says that sequence diagrams are better when you want to emphasize the sequence of calls and that communication diagrams are better when you want to emphasize the links. Many people find that communication diagrams are easier to alter on a whiteboard, so they are a good approach for exploring alternatives, although in those cases, I often prefer CRC cards.

Chapter 13

Composite Structures

One of the most significant new features in UML 2 is the ability to hierarchically decompose a class into an internal structure. This allows you to take a complex object and break it down into parts.

Figure 13.1 shows a TV Viewer class with its provided and required interfaces (page 69). I've shown this in two ways: using the ball-and-socket notation and listing them internally.

Figure 13.2 shows how this class is decomposed internally into two parts and which parts support and require the different interfaces. Each part is named in the form name : class, with both elements individually optional. Parts are not instance specifications, so they are bolded rather than underlined.

You can show how many instances of a part are present. Figure 13.2 says that each TV Viewer contains one generator part and one controls part.

To show a part implementing an interface, you draw a delegation connector from that interface. Similarly, to show that a part needs an interface, you show a delegation connector to that interface. You can also show connectors between parts with either a simple line, as I've done here, or with ball-and-socket notation (page 140).

You can add ports (Figure 13.3) to the external structure. Ports allow you to group the required and provided interfaces into logical interactions that a component has with the outside world.

135

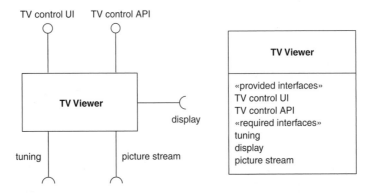

Figure 13.1 *Two ways of showing a TV viewer and its interfaces*

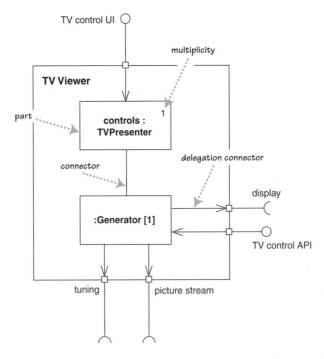

Figure 13.2 *Internal view of a component (example suggested by Jim Rumbaugh)*

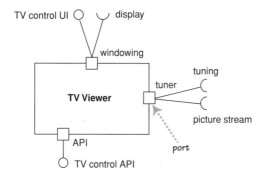

Figure 13.3 *A component with multiple ports*

When to Use Composite Structures

Composite structures are new to UML 2, although some older methods had some similar ideas. A good way of thinking about the difference between packages and composite structures is that packages are a compile-time grouping, while composite structures show runtime groupings. As such, they are a natural fit for showing components and how they are broken into parts; hence, much of this notation is used in component diagrams.

Because composite structures are new to the UML, it's too early to tell how effective they will turn out in practice; many members of the UML committee think that these diagrams will become a very valuable addition.

Chapter 14

Component Diagrams

A debate that's always ranged large in the OO community is what the difference is between a component and any regular class. This is not a debate that I want to settle here, but I can show you the notation the UML uses to distinguish between them.

UML 1 had a distinctive symbol for a component (Figure 14.1). UML 2 removed that icon but allows you to annotate a class box with a similar-looking icon. Alternatively, you can use the «component» keyword.

Other than the icon, components don't introduce any notation that we haven't already seen. Components are connected through implemented and required interfaces and often use the notations from Composite Structures that we saw in Chapter 13.

Figure 14.2 shows an example component diagram. In this example sales tills connect to the sales servers component using a sales message interface via a message queue. The queue supplies both the sales message interface to talk with the till and requires that interface to talk with the server. The server is broken down into two major components: the transaction processor realizes the sales message interface and the accounting driver talks to the accounting system.

In all cases these components are shown as parts of a wider retail system, hence the leading colons. Multiplicity markers indicate that there are many tills and servers, but only one queue and accounting system. If you don't show a multiplicity, as I haven't for the internals of the sales server, it's assumed to be one. In general I prefer to explicitly show the multiplicity if it's of any importance. You can use either the ball-and-socket notation or simple lines for the connectors. The ball and socket is useful to show an interface, otherwise a simple line is easier to draw.

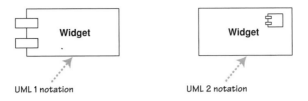

Figure 14.1 *Notation for components*

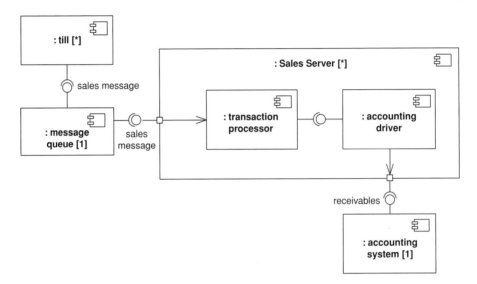

Figure 14.2 *An example component diagram*

Figure 14.2 is in the style of a Composite Structure Diagram. Indeed I think of it as the same as a Composite Structure Diagram, but with a minor adornment that makes the parts components. You can also draw Component Diagrams in the form of class diagrams—usually these focus on the dependencies between the components. A good way to think of this is that component class diagrams show the possible connection between components, while the component composite structure shows the actual connections between components in a specific context.

As I've already said, the issue of what is a component is the subject of endless debate. One of the more helpful statements I've found is this:

Components are not a technology. Technology people seem to find this hard to understand. Components are about how customers want to relate to software. They want to be able to buy their software a piece at a time, and to be able to upgrade it just like they can upgrade their stereo. They want new pieces to work seamlessly with their old pieces, and to be able to upgrade on their own schedule, not the manufacturer's schedule. They want to be able to mix and match pieces from various manufacturers. This is a very reasonable requirement. It is just hard to satisfy.

Ralph Johnson, **http://www.c2.com/cgi/wiki?DoComponentsExist**

The important point is that components represent pieces that are independently purchasable and upgradeable. As a result, dividing a system into components is as much a marketing decision as it is a technical decision, for which [Hohmann] is an excellent guide. It's also a reminder to beware of overly fine-grained components, because too many components are hard to manage, especially when versioning rears its ugly head, hence "DLL hell."

In earlier versions of the UML, components were used to represent physical structures, such as DLLs. That's no longer true; for this task, you now use artifacts (page 97).

When to Use Component Diagrams

Use component diagrams when you are dividing your system into components and want to show their interrelationships through interfaces or the breakdown of components into a lower-level structure.

Chapter 15

Collaborations

Unlike the other chapters in this book, this one does not correspond to an official diagram in UML 2. The standard discusses collaborations as part of composite structures, but the diagram is really quite different and was used in UML 1 without any link to composite structures. So I felt it best to discuss collaborations as their own chapter.

Let's consider the notion of an auction. In any auction, we might have a seller, some buyers, a lot of goods, and some offers for the sale. We can describe these elements in terms of a class diagram (Figure 15.1) and perhaps some interaction diagrams (Figure 15.2).

Figure 15.1 is not quite a regular class diagram. For a start, it's surrounded by the dashed ellipse, which represents the auction collaboration. Second, the so-called classes in the collaboration are not classes but **roles** that will be realized as the collaboration is applied—hence the fact that their names aren't capitalized. It's not unusual to see actual interfaces or classes that correspond to the collaboration roles, but you don't have to have them.

In the interaction diagram, the participants are labeled slightly differently from the usual case. In a collaboration, the naming scheme is `participant-name / role-name : class-name`. As usual, all these elements are optional.

When you use a collaboration, you can show you're using one by placing a **collaboration occurrence** on a class diagram, as in Figure 15.3, a class diagram of some of the classes in the application. The links from the collaboration to those classes indicate how the classes play the various roles defined in the collaboration.

The UML suggests that you can use the collaboration occurrence notation to show the use of patterns, but hardly any patterns author has done this. Erich Gamma developed a nice alternative notation (Figure 15.4). Elements of the diagram are labeled with either the pattern name or a combination of `pattern:role`.

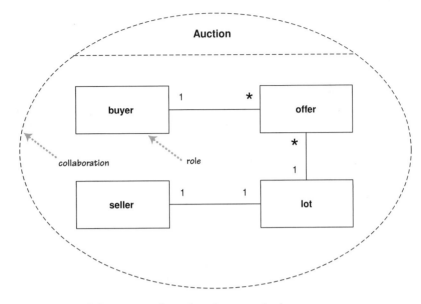

Figure 15.1 *A collaboration with its class diagram of roles*

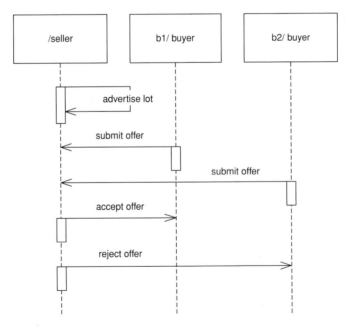

Figure 15.2 *A sequence diagram for the auction collaboration*

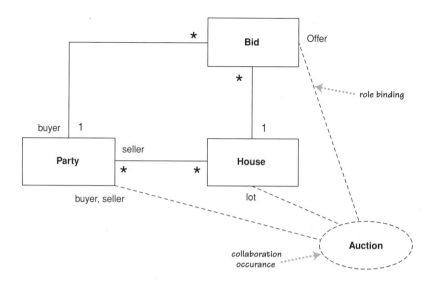

Figure 15.3 *A collaboration occurrence*

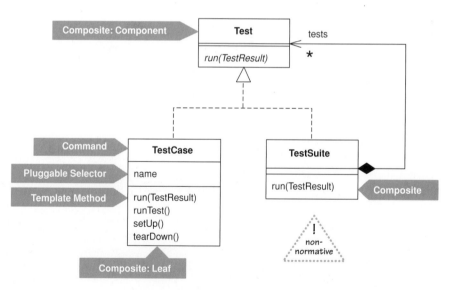

Figure 15.4 *A nonstandard way of showing pattern use in JUnit (junit.org)*

When to Use Collaborations

Collaborations have been around since UML 1, but I admit I've hardly used them, even in my patterns writing. Collaborations do provide a way to group chunks of interaction behavior when roles are played by different classes. In practice, however, I've not found that they've been a compelling diagram type.

Chapter 16

Interaction Overview Diagrams

Interaction overview diagrams are a grafting together of activity diagrams and sequence diagrams. You can think of interaction overview diagrams either as activity diagrams in which the activities are replaced by little sequence diagrams, or as a sequence diagram broken up with activity diagram notation used to show control flow. Either way, they make a bit of an odd mixture.

Figure 16.1 shows a simple example of one; the notation is familiar from what you've already seen in the activity diagram and sequence diagram chapters. In this diagram, we want to produce and format an order summary report. If the customer is external, we get the information from XML; if internal, we get it from a database. Small sequence diagrams show the two alternatives. Once we get the data, we format the report; in this case, we don't show the sequence diagram but simply reference it with a reference interaction frame.

When to Use Interaction Overview Diagrams

These are new for UML 2, and it's too early to get much sense of how well they will work out in practice. I'm not keen on them, as I think that they mix two styles that don't really mix that well. Either draw an activity diagram or use a sequence diagram, depending on what better serves your purpose.

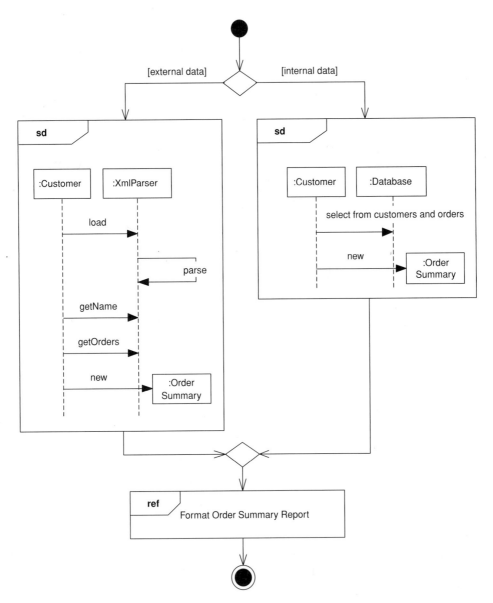

Figure 16.1 *Interaction overview diagram*

Chapter 17

Timing Diagrams

After leaving secondary school, I started out in electronic engineering before I switched into computing. So I feel a certain anguished familiarity when I see the UML define timing diagrams as one of its standard diagrams. Timing diagrams have been around in electronic engineering for a long time and never seemed to need the UML's help to define their meaning. But since they are in the UML, they deserve a brief mention.

Timing diagrams are another form of interaction diagram, where the focus is on timing constraints: either for a single object or, more usefully, for a bunch of objects. Let's take a simple scenario based on the pump and hotplate for a coffee pot. Let's imagine a rule that says that at least 10 seconds must pass between the pump coming on and the hotplate coming on. When the water reservoir becomes empty, the pump switches off, and the hotplate cannot stay on for more than 15 minutes more.

Figures 17.1 and 17.2 are alternative ways of showing these timing constraints. Both diagrams show the same basic information. The main difference is that Figure 17.1 shows the state changes by moving from one horizontal line to another, while Figure 17.2 retains the same horizontal position but shows state changes with a cross. The style of Figure 17.1 works better when there are just a few states, as in this case, and Figure 17.2 is better when there are many states to deal with.

The dashed lines that I've used on the {>10s} constraints are optional. Use them if you think they help clarify exactly what events the timing constrains.

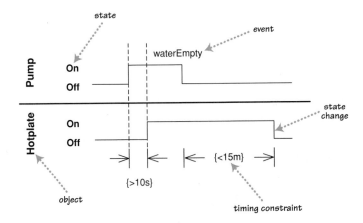

Figure 17.1 *Timing diagram showing states as lines*

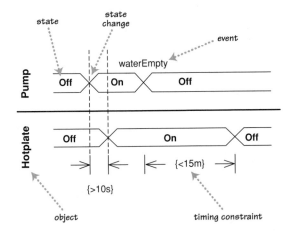

Figure 17.2 *Timing diagram showing states as areas*

When to Use Timing Diagrams

Timing diagrams are useful for showing timing constraints between state changes on different objects. The diagrams are particularly familiar to hardware engineers.

Appendix

Changes between UML Versions

When the first edition of this book appeared on the shelves, the UML was in version 1.0. Much of it appeared to have stabilized and was in the process of OMG recognition. Since then, there have been a number of revisions. In this appendix, I describe the significant changes that have occurred since 1.0 and how those changes affect the material in this book.

This appendix summarizes the changes so you can keep up to date if you have an earlier printing of the book. I have made changes to the book to keep up with the UML, so if you have a later printing, it describes the situation as it was as of the print date.

Revisions to the UML

The earliest public release of what came to be the UML was version 0.8 of the Unified Method, which was released for OOPSLA in October 1995. This was the work of Booch and Rumbaugh, as Jacobson did not join Rational until around that time. In 1996, Rational released versions 0.9 and 0.91, which included Jacobson's work. After the latter version, they changed the name to the UML.

Rational and a group of partners submitted version 1.0 of the UML to the OMG Analysis and Design Task Force in January 1997. Subsequently, the Rational partnership and the other submitters combined their work and submitted a single proposal for the OMG standard in September 1997, for version 1.1 of the UML. This was adopted by the OMG toward the end of 1997. However, in a fit of darkest obfuscation, the OMG called this standard version 1.0. So, now the UML was both OMG version 1.0 and Rational version 1.1, not to be confused with Rational 1.0. In practice, everyone calls that standard version 1.1.

From then on, there were a number of further developments in the UML. UML 1.2 appeared in 1998, 1.3 in 1999, 1.4 in 2001, and 1.5 in 2003. Most of the changes between the 1.x versions were fairly deep in the UML, except for UML 1.3, which caused some very visible changes, especially to use cases and activity diagrams.

As the UML 1 series continued, the developers of the UML set their sights on a major revision to the UML with UML 2. The first RFPs (Request for Proposals) were issued in 2000, but UML 2 didn't start to properly stabilize until 2003.

Further developments in the UML will almost certainly occur. The UML Forum (**http://uml-forum.com**) is usually a good place to look for more information. I also keep some UML information on my site (**http://martinfowler.com**).

Changes in *UML Distilled*

As these revisions go on, I've been trying to keep up by revising *UML Distilled* with subsequent printings. I've also taken the opportunity to fix errors and make clarifications.

The most dynamic period for keeping up with things was during the first edition of *UML Distilled*, when we often had to make updates between printings to keep up with the emerging UML standard. The first through fifth printings were based on UML 1.0. Any changes to the UML between these printings were minor. The sixth printing took UML 1.1 into account.

The seventh through tenth printings were based on UML 1.2; the eleventh printing was the first to use UML 1.3. Printings based on versions of the UML after 1.0 have the UML version number on the front cover.

The first though sixth printings of the second edition were based on version 1.3. The seventh printing was the first to take into account the minor changes of version 1.4.

The third edition was launched to update the book with UML 2 (see Table A.1). In the rest of this appendix, I summarize the major changes in the UML from 1.0 to 1.1, from 1.2 to 1.3, and from 1.x to 2.0. I don't discuss all the changes that occur but rather only those that change something I said in *UML Distilled* or that represent important features that I would have discussed in *UML Distilled*.

I am continuing to follow the spirit of *UML Distilled*: to discuss the key elements of UML as they affect the application of the UML within real-world projects. As ever, the selections and advice are my own. If there is any conflict between what I say and the official UML documents, the UML documents are the ones to follow. (But do let me know, so I can make corrections.)

Table A.1 UML Distilled *and corresponding UML versions*

UML Distilled	UML Versions
1st edition	UML 1.0–1.3
2nd edition	UML 1.3–1.4
3rd edition	UML 2.0 onward

I have also taken the opportunity to indicate any important errors and omissions in the earlier printings. Thanks to the readers who have pointed these out to me.

Changes from UML 1.0 to 1.1

Type and Implementation Class

In the first edition of *UML Distilled*, I talked about perspectives and how they altered the way people draw and interpret models—in particular, class diagrams. UML now takes this into account by saying that all classes on a class diagram can be specialized as either types or implementation classes.

An **implementation class** corresponds to a class in the software environment in which you are developing. A **type** is rather more nebulous; it represents a less implementation-bound abstraction. This could be a CORBA type, a specification perspective of a class, or a conceptual perspective. If necessary, you can add stereotypes to differentiate further.

You can state that for a particular diagram, all classes follow a particular stereotype. This is what you would do when drawing a diagram from a particular perspective. The implementation perspective would use implementation classes, whereas the specification and conceptual perspective would use types.

You use the realization relationship to indicate that an implementation class implements one or more types.

There is a distinction between type and interface. An interface is intended to directly correspond to a Java or COM-style interface. Interfaces thus have only operations and no attributes.

You may use only single, static classification with implementation classes, but you can use multiple and dynamic classification with types. (I assume that this is because the major OO languages follow single, static classification. If one fine day you use a language that supports multiple or dynamic classification, that restriction really should not apply.)

Complete and Incomplete Discriminator Constraints

In previous printings of *UML Distilled*, I said that the {complete} constraint on a generalization indicated that all instances of the supertype must also be an instance of a subtype within that partition. UML 1.1 defines instead that {complete} indicates that all subtypes within that partition have been specified, which is not quite the same thing. I have found some inconsistency on the interpretation of this constraint, so you should be wary of it. If you do want to indicate that all instances of the supertype should be an instance of one of the subtypes, I suggest using another constraint to avoid confusion. Currently, I am using {mandatory}.

Composition

In UML 1.0, using composition implied that the link was immutable, or frozen, at least for single-valued components. That constraint is no longer part of the definition.

Immutability and Frozen

UML defines the constraint {frozen} to define immutability on association roles. As it's currently defined, it doesn't seem to apply it to attributes or classes. In my practice, I now use the term **frozen** instead of immutability, and I'm happy to apply the constraint to association roles, classes, and attributes.

Returns on Sequence Diagrams

In UML 1.0, a return on a sequence diagram was distinguished by using a stick arrowhead instead of a solid arrowhead (see previous printings). This was something of a pain, as the distinction was too subtle and easy to miss. UML 1.1 uses a dashed arrow for a return, which pleases me, as it makes returns much more obvious. (As I used dashed returns in *Analysis Patterns* [Fowler, AP], it also makes me look influential.) You can name what is returned for later use by using the form enoughStock := check().

Use of the Term "Role"

In UML 1.0, the term **role** indicated primarily a direction on an association (see previous printings). UML 1.1 refers to this usage as an **association role**. There is also a **collaboration role**, which is a role that an instance of a class plays in a collaboration. UML 1.1 gives a lot more emphasis to collaborations, and it looks as though this use of "role" may become the primary one.

Changes from UML 1.2 (and 1.1) to 1.3 (and 1.5)

Use Cases

The changes to use cases involve new relationships between use cases. UML 1.1 has two use case relationships: «uses» and «extends», both of which are stereotypes of generalization. UML 1.3 offers three relationships.

- The «include» construct is a stereotype of dependency. This indicates that the path of one use case is included in another. Typically, this occurs when a few use cases share common steps. The included use case can factor out the common behavior. An example from an ATM might be that Withdraw Money and Make Transfer both use Validate Customer. This replaces the common use of «uses».

- Use case **generalization** indicates that one use case is a variation on another. Thus, we might have one use case for Withdraw Money—the base use case—and a separate use case to handle the case when the withdrawal is refused because of lack of funds. The refusal could be handled as a use case that specializes the withdrawal use case. (You could also handle it as simply another scenario within the Withdraw Money use case.) A specializing use case like this may change any aspect of the base use case.

- The «extend» construct is a stereotype of dependency. This provides a more controlled form of extension than the generalization relationship. Here, the base use case declares a number of extension points. The extending use case can alter behavior only at those extension points. So, if you are buying a product on line, you might have a use case for buying a product with extension points for capturing the shipping information and capturing payment information. That use case could then be extended for a regular customer for which this information would be obtained in a different way.

There is some confusion about the relationship between the old relationships and the new ones. Most people used «uses» the way the 1.3 «includes» is used, so for most people, we can say that «includes» replaces «uses». And most people used 1.1 «extends» in both the controlled manner of the 1.3 «extends» and as a general overriding in the style of the 1.3 generalization. So, you can think that 1.1 «extends» has been split into the 1.3 «extend» and generalization.

Now, although this explanation covers most UML usage that I've seen, it isn't the strictly correct way of using those old relationships. However, most people didn't follow the strict usage, and I don't really want to get into all that here.

Activity Diagrams

When the UML reached version 1.2, there were quite a few open questions about the semantics of activity diagrams. So, the 1.3 effort involved quite a lot of tightening up on these semantics.

For conditional behavior, you can now use the diamond-shaped decision activity for a merge of behavior as well as a branch. Although neither branches nor merges are necessary to describe conditional behavior, it is increasingly common style to show them so that you can bracket conditional behavior.

The synchronization bar is now referred to as a **fork**—when splitting control—or as a **join**—when synchronizing control together. However, you can no longer add arbitrary conditions to joins. Also, you must follow matching rules to ensure that forks and joins match up. Essentially, this means that each fork must have a corresponding join that joins the threads started by that fork. You can nest fork and joins, though, and you can eliminate forks and joins on the diagram when threads go directly from one fork to another fork, or one join to another join.

Joins are fired only when all incoming threads complete. However, you can have a condition on a thread coming out of a fork. If that condition is false, that thread is considered complete for joining purposes.

The multiple-trigger feature is no longer present. In its place, you can have dynamic concurrency in an activity, shown with a * inside an activity box. Such an activity may be invoked several times in parallel; all its invocations must complete before any outgoing transition can be taken. This is loosely equivalent to, although less flexible than, a multiple trigger and matching synchronization condition.

These rules reduce some of flexibility of activity diagrams but do ensure that activity diagrams are truly special cases of state machines. The relationship between activity diagrams and state machines was a matter of some debate in the RTF.

Changes from UML 1.3 to 1.4

The most visible change in UML 1.4 is the addition of **profiles**, which allows a group of extensions to be collected together into a coherent set. The UML documentation includes a couple of example profiles. Together with this, there's greater formalism involved in defining a stereotype, and model elements can now have multiple stereotypes; they were limited to one stereotype in UML 1.3.

Artifacts were added to the UML. An artifact is a physical manifestation of a component, so, for example, Xerces is a component and all those copies of the Xerces jar on my disk drive are artifacts that implement the Xerces component.

Prior to 1.3, there was nothing in the UML meta-model to handle Java's **package visibility**. Now there is, and the symbol is "~".

UML 1.4 also made the stick arrowhead in interaction diagrams mark asynchronous, a rather awkward backward-incompatible change. That caught out a few people, including me.

Changes from UML 1.4. to 1.5

The principal change here was adding action semantics to the UML, a necessary step to make UML a programming language. This was done to allow people to work on this without waiting for the full UML 2.

From UML 1.x to UML 2.0

UML 2 represents the biggest change that's happened yet to the UML. All sorts of things have changed with this revision, and many changes have affected *UML Distilled*.

Within the UML, there have been deep changes to the UML meta-model. Although these changes don't affect the discussion in *UML Distilled*, they are very important to some groups.

One of the most obvious changes is the introduction of new diagram types. Object diagrams and package diagrams were widely drawn before but weren't official diagram types; now they are. UML 2 changed the name of collaboration diagrams to communication diagrams. UML 2 has also introduced new diagram types: interaction overview diagrams, timing diagrams, and composite structure diagrams.

A lot of changes haven't touched *UML Distilled*. I've left out discussion of such constructs as state machine extensions, gates in interactions diagrams, and power types in class diagrams.

So for this section, I'm discussing only changes that make it into *UML Distilled*. These are either changes to things I discussed in previous editions or new things I've started to discuss with this edition. Because the changes are so widespread, I've organized them according to the chapters in this book.

Class Diagrams: The Essentials (Chapter 3)

Attributes and unidirectional associations are now primarily simply different notations for the same underlying concept of property. Discontinuous multiplicities, such as [2, 4], have been dropped. The frozen property has been dropped. I've added a list of common dependency keywords, several of which are new to UML 2. The «parameter», and «local» keywords have been dropped.

Sequence Diagrams (Chapter 4)

The big change here is the interaction frame notation for sequence diagrams to handle iterative, conditional, and various other controls of behavior. This now allows you to express algorithms pretty completely in sequence diagrams, although I'm not convinced that these are any clearer than code. The old iteration markers and guards on messages have been dropped from sequence diagrams. The heads of the lifelines are no longer instances; I use the term **participant** to refer to them. The collaboration diagrams of UML 1 were renamed to communication diagrams for UML 2.

Class Diagrams: Concepts (Chapter 5)

Stereotypes are now more tightly defined. As a result, I now refer to words in guillemets as keywords, only some of which are stereotypes. Instances on object diagrams are now instance specifications. Classes can now require interfaces as well as provide them. Multiple classification uses generalization sets to group generalizations into groups. Components are no longer drawn with their special symbol. Active objects have double vertical lines instead of thick lines.

State Machine Diagrams (Chapter 10)

UML 1 separated short-lived actions from long-lived activities. UML 2 calls both activities and uses the term do-activity for the long-lived activities.

Activity Diagrams (Chapter 11)

UML 1 treated activity diagrams as a special case of state diagram. UML 2 broke that link and as a result removed the rules of matching forks and joins that UML 1 activity diagrams had to keep to. As a result, they are best understood by token flow rather than by state transition. A whole bunch of new notation thus appeared, including time and accept signals, parameters, join specifications, pins, flow transformations, subdiagram rakes, expansion regions, and flow finals.

A simple but awkward change is that UML 1 treated multiple incoming flows to an activity as an implicit merge, while UML 2 treats them as an implicit join. For this reason, I advise using an explicit merge or join when doing activity diagrams.

Swim lanes can now be multidimensional and are generally called partitions.

Bibliography

[Ambler]
Scott Ambler, *Agile Modeling*, Wiley, 2002.

[Beck]
Kent Beck, *Extreme Programming Explained: Embrace Change*, Addison-Wesley, 2000.

[Beck and Fowler]
Kent Beck and Martin Fowler, *Planning Extreme Programming*, Addison-Wesley, 2000.

[Beck and Cunningham]
Kent Beck and Ward Cunningham, "A Laboratory for Teaching Object-Oriented Thinking," *Proceedings of OOPSLA 89*, 24 (10): 1–6. **http://c2.com/doc/oopsla89/paper.html**

[Booch, OOAD]
Grady Booch, *Object-Oriented Analysis and Design with Applications, Second Edition*. Addison-Wesley, 1994.

[Booch, UML user]
Grady Booch, Jim Rumbaugh, and Ivar Jacobson, *UML User Guide*, Addison-Wesley, 1999.

[Coad, OOA]
Peter Coad and Edward Yourdon, *Object-Oriented Analysis*, Yourdon Press, 1991.

[Coad, OOD]
Peter Coad and Edward Yourdon, *Object-Oriented Design*, Yourdon Press, 1991.

[Cockburn, agile]
Alistair Cockburn, *Agile Software Development*, Addison-Wesley, 2001.

[Cockburn, use cases]
Alistair Cockburn, *Writing Effective Use Cases*, Addison-Wesley, 2001.

[Constantine and Lockwood]
Larry Constantine and Lucy Lockwood, *Software for Use*, Addison-Wesley, 2000.

[Cook and Daniels]
Steve Cook and John Daniels, *Designing Object Systems: Object-Oriented Modeling with Syntropy*, Prentice-Hall, 1994.

[Core J2EE Patterns]
Deepak Alur, John Crupi, and Dan Malks, *Core J2EE Patterns*, Prentice-Hall, 2001.

[Cunningham]
Ward Cunningham, "EPISODES: A Pattern Language of Competitive Development." In *Pattern Languages of Program Design 2*, Vlissides, Coplien, and Kerth, Addison-Wesley, 1996, pp. 371–388.

[Douglass]
Bruce Powel Douglass, *Real-Time UML*, Addison-Wesley, 1999.

[Fowler, AP]
Martin Fowler, *Analysis Patterns: Reusable Object Models*, Addison-Wesley, 1997.

[Fowler, new methodology]
Martin Fowler, "The New Methodology," **http://martinfowler.com/articles/newMethodology.html**

[Fowler and Foemmel]
Martin Fowler and Matthew Foemmel, "Continuous Integration," **http://martinfowler.com/articles/continuousIntegration.html**

[Fowler, P of EAA]

Martin Fowler, *Patterns of Enterprise Application Architecture*, Addison-Wesley, 2003.

[Fowler, refactoring]

Martin Fowler, *Refactoring: Improving the Design of Existing Programs*, Addison-Wesley, 1999.

[Gang of Four]

Erich Gamma, Richard Helm, Ralph Johnson, and John Vlissides, *Design Patterns: Elements of Reusable Object-Oriented Software*, Addison-Wesley, 1995.

[Highsmith]

Jim Highsmith, *Agile Software Development Ecosystems*, Addison-Wesley, 2002.

[Hohmann]

Luke Hohmann, *Beyond Software Architecture*, Addison-Wesley, 2003.

[Jacobson, OOSE]

Ivar Jacobson, Magnus Christerson, Patrik Jonsson, and Gunnar Övergaard, *Object-Oriented Software Engineering: A Use Case Driven Approach*, Addison-Wesley, 1992.

[Jacobson, UP]

Ivar Jacobson, Maria Ericsson, and Agneta Jacobson, *The Object Advantage: Business Process Reengineering with Object Technology*, Addison-Wesley, 1995.

[Kerth]

Norm Kerth, *Project Retrospectives*, Dorset House, 2001

[Kleppe et al.]

Anneke Kleppe, Jos Warmer, and Wim Bast, *MDA Explained*, Addison-Wesley, 2003.

[Kruchten]

Philippe Kruchten, *The Rational Unified Process: An Introduction*, Addison-Wesley, 1999.

[Larman]

Craig Larman, *Applying UML and Patterns*, 2d ed., Prentice-Hall, 2001.

[Martin]

Robert Cecil Martin, *The Principles, Patterns, and Practices of Agile Software Development,* Prentice-Hall, 2003.

[McConnell]

Steve McConnell, *Rapid Development: Taming Wild Software Schedules,* Microsoft Press, 1996.

[Mellor and Balcer]

Steve Mellor and Marc Balcer, *Executable UML*, Addison-Wesley, 2002.

[Meyer]

Bertrand Meyer, *Object-Oriented Software Construction*. Prentice-Hall, 2000.

[Odell]

James Martin and James J. Odell, *Object-Oriented Methods: A Foundation (UML Edition)*, Prentice Hall, 1998.

[Pont]

Michael Pont, *Patterns for Time-Triggered Embedded Systems*, Addison-Wesley, 2001.

[POSA1]

Frank Buschmann, Regine Meunier, Hans Rohnert, Peter Sommerlad, and Michael Stal, *Pattern-Oriented Software Architecture: A System of Patterns,* Wiley, 1996.

[POSA2]

Douglas Schmidt, Michael Stal, Hans Rohnert, and Frank Buschmann, *Pattern-Oriented Software Archtecture Volume 2: Patterns for Concurrent and Networked Objects*, Wiley, 2000.

[Rumbaugh, insights]

James Rumbaugh, *OMT Insights*, SIGS Books, 1996.

[Rumbaugh, OMT]

James Rumbaugh, Michael Blaha, William Premerlani, Frederick Eddy, and William Lorenzen, *Object-Oriented Modeling and Design*, Prentice-Hall, 1991.

[Rumbaugh, UML Reference]

James Rumbaugh, Ivar Jacobson, and Grady Booch, *The Unified Modeling Language Reference Manual*, Addison-Wesley, 1999.

[Shlaer and Mellor, data]

Sally Shlaer and Stephen J. Mellor, *Object-Oriented Systems Analysis: Modeling the World in Data*, Yourdon Press, 1989.

[Shlaer and Mellor, states]

Sally Shlaer and Stephen J. Mellor, *Object Lifecycles: Modeling the World in States*. Yourdon Press, 1991.

[Warmer and Kleppe]

Jos Warmer and Anneke Kleppe, *The Object Constraint Language: Precise Modeling with UML*, Addison-Wesley, 1998.

[Wirfs-Brock]

Rebecca Wirfs-Brock and Alan McKean, *Object Design: Roles Responsibilities and Collaborations*. Addison-Wesley, 2003.

Index

Also by Martin Fowler

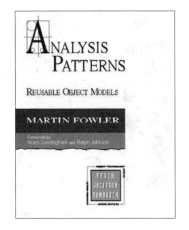

0201895420

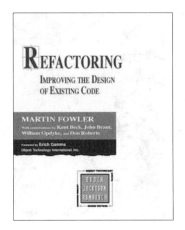

0201485672

0201710919

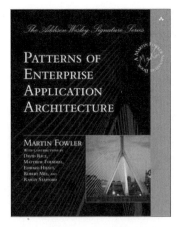

0321127420

For more information about these and other titles, please visit **www.awprofessional.com**

Package Diagram *p. 89*

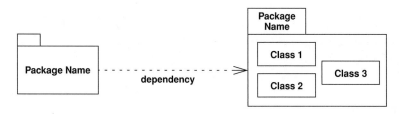

Package Name — — — dependency — — —▷

Package Name

Class 1

Class 2

Class 3

Activity Diagram *p. 117*

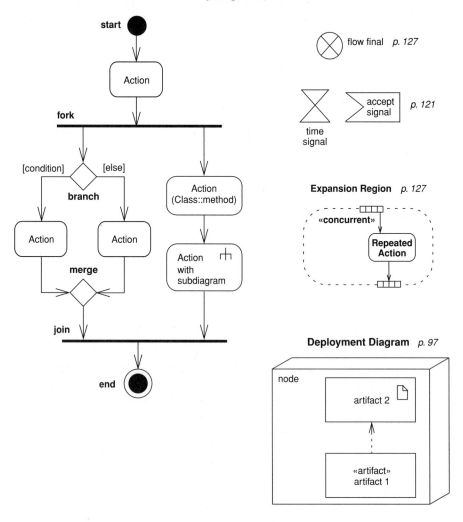

start

Action

fork

[condition]   [else]

branch

Action   Action

merge

join

end

Action
(Class::method)

Action
with
subdiagram

flow final *p. 127*

time
signal

accept
signal

p. 121

Expansion Region *p. 127*

«concurrent»

Repeated
Action

Deployment Diagram *p. 97*

node

artifact 2

«artifact»
artifact 1